YORK NOTES

General Editors: Professor A.N. Jeffares (*University of Stirling*) & Professor Suheil Bushrui (*American University of Beirut*)

James Joyce

DUBLINERS

Notes by Patrick Rafroidi

AGRÉGÉ D'ANGLAIS, DOCTEUR-ÈS-LETTRES (SORBONNE)
*Professor at the University of
Paris III – Sorbonne Nouvelle*

LONGMAN
YORK PRESS

YORK PRESS
Immeuble Esseily, Place Riad Solh, Beirut.

ADDISON WESLEY LONGMAN LIMITED
Edinburgh Gate, Harlow,
Essex CM20 2JE, England
Associated companies, branches and representatives
throughout the world

© Librairie du Liban 1985

First published 1985
Fourteenth impression 1997

ISBN 0-582-78215-5

Produced by Longman Singapore Publishers Pte Ltd
Printed in Singapore

Contents

Part 1

Introduction

Joyce's life and works

James Joyce was born on 2 February 1882 in Rathgar, a south Dublin suburb, the oldest boy among the ten children of John Stanislaus Joyce (1849–1931)—an improvident rate collector and 'praiser of his own past', ever present in James's works from *Dubliners* to *Finnegans Wake* (where he is called 'Earwicker')—and Mary Jane ('Mae') Murray (1859–1903). James was baptised in the Roman Catholic faith on 5 February at the church of St Joseph, Terenure.

In 1887 the Joyce family moved to Bray, a seaside town fifteen miles south of Dublin, where they were joined by Mrs 'Dante' Hearn Conway from Cork. Mrs Conway was to act as governess to the children and play an important part in the Christmas scene of *Portrait of the Artist*. From 1888 to 1891 Joyce studied at Clongowes Wood College, Sallins, County Kildare, a well-known Jesuit school. In 1891, on the occasion of the death of Charles Stewart Parnell ('the uncrowned king of Ireland') on 6 October—henceforth to become 'Ivy Day'—Joyce composed his first printed work, in honour of the hero: *Et Tu, Healy*.

In 1892 the family, in financial difficulty, moved first to Blackrock and then to Dublin city. After a brief interlude with the Christian Brothers on North Richmond Street, Joyce resumed his Jesuit schooling—without fees—at Belvedere College. He was to remain there from 6 April 1893, until 1898. In 1898 he entered University College, Dublin, where he read French, Italian and English, and made friends with George Clancy, Vincent Cosgrave, Francis Skeffington, Thomas Kettle, John Francis Byrne, Oliver Gogarty and others. On 1 April 1900, the *Fortnightly Review* published his essay 'Ibsen's New Drama' for which the playwright wrote to thank Joyce. The following year, *St Stephen's* refused another essay, attacking the Irish Literary Theatre: 'The Day of the Rabblement'. This was privately printed in November 1901.

In 1902, Joyce left for Paris in order to study medicine, although he soon returned to Dublin. His second trip to Paris in 1903 was cut short in April when he received a telegram: 'Mother dying come home. Father'. Mrs Joyce died in August.

In 1904 Joyce started work on the first draft of *Stephen Hero*. During that year he fell in love with Nora Barnacle, a Galway girl who worked at Finn's Hotel in Dublin. He took her out on 16 June (the day of *Ulysses*).

On 13 August he published the first story of *Dubliners*, 'The Sisters', in A.E.'s (George Russell's) *Irish Homestead*. In September he stayed at the Sandycove Martello Tower with Oliver Gogarty and a man named Samuel Trench, but soon quarrelled with them. In October Joyce departed with Nora to Zurich, where he expected to teach at the Berlitz school. As the position was not available however, he took another one in Pola. In 1905 he obtained a teaching post in Trieste where he carried on with the composition of *Dubliners*. His son, Giorgio, was born on 27 July 1905. Soon after this Joyce was joined in Trieste by his brother Stanislaus, on whom he was to depend heavily for financial support for many years to come. It was in December of that year that he sent the twelve stories of *Dubliners* to the publisher Grant Richards. Although the manuscript was accepted, difficulties arose with the printer in 1906. Joyce was now in Rome where he worked in a bank—a job he disliked. By February 1907 he was back in Trieste. That year saw the publication of Joyce's poems under the title *Chamber Music* and the birth of a daughter, Lucia Anna.

The next six years were marked by the beginning of Joyce's eye troubles; his last two trips to Ireland—to Dublin in 1909 (where he suffered an acute attack of jealousy, to be remembered in *Exiles*) and to Galway and Dublin in 1912; and the start of his correspondence with Ezra Pound in 1913. In 1914 *A Portrait of the Artist as a Young Man* was published serially in the *The Egoist* (the work was published in book form in 1916, in New York). In 1907 *Dubliners* had been rejected by Richards; it was then accepted and rejected by Maunsel, the Dublin publishing company with which Joyce had signed a contract for it in 1909; and finally taken up again by Richards and published in London.

In 1915 the Joyces moved to Zurich; they returned to Trieste in 1919, and then chose Paris as their residence in 1920. Joyce's play *Exiles* was published in 1918 in London and New York, where *The Little Review* began to serialise *Ulysses*. But it was not until 1922 that the full text was published in book form, in Paris. The French translation, in which Joyce assisted, appeared in 1929.

In 1923 Joyce started *Work in Progress* (which became *Finnegans Wake*), the first fragments of which were published in Paris the following year, in Ford Madox Ford's *Transatlantic Review*. Most of the book was subsequently published in various magazines. His second collection of poems, *Pomes Penyeach*, was published in 1927.

On 4 July 1931 Joyce and Nora were married in London 'for testamentary reasons'. Their son Giorgio was married the same year to Helen Kastor Fleischmann, and a grandson, Stephen, was born in 1932. Their daughter Lucia's mental health began to deteriorate and she had to be placed under medical care. On 29 December 1931, Joyce's father died in Dublin. By 1933 Joyce had become nearly blind. During that year, however, he had the pleasure of hearing that *Ulysses*— previously banned in all English-speaking countries—had been judged not obscene in New York and the American version authorised.

Two more of Joyce's books were published in the thirties: his *Collected Poems* (1936) and *Finnegans Wake* (1939). In December 1940 Joyce and Nora fled from 'Vichy' France to Switzerland. Joyce died on 13 January 1941, in Zurich, of a perforated ulcer.

The backgrounds of *Dubliners*

The Irish tradition of storytelling

The Irishness of *Dubliners* has more aspects than the place described, the inhabitants portrayed, or the origins of the author. For *Dubliners* is a collection of stories, a genre exceptionally popular in Ireland, which is heir to the immemorial national tradition of the oral tale told by a professional storyteller: in Gaelic *sgéalaí* (the specialist of the long mythological narrative, *sean-sgeal*) or *seanchaí* (who dealt with shorter stories: *eachtra* and *seanchas*). Every year, from Hallowe'en (31 October) to the night of St Patrick's Day (17 March), such storytellers were the very soul of the *céili*—a gathering of people around the fireplace, in mansions or cottages—where their performance was drawn from a repertory of three hundred and fifty items or more.

The genre developed from voice to writing, from Gaelic to English, from legend to modern short story, which resembles its ancestor in its frequent reliance on the testimony of the author. Even in its modern guise, the Irish short story had its masters before Joyce; they are, perhaps, more relevant to an understanding of his craft than such figures as Maupassant (1850–93) in France, or Chekhov (1860–94) in Russia. Joyce may be, in many ways, a beginning; but he is also an end. Besides, the existence of a long-standing tradition of story-telling is not the only reason why Irishmen before Joyce (and Joyce himself) should have preferred the shorter type of narrative. From a sociological point of view, there is no doubt that the short story, more than the novel, can easily become the voice of those whom Frank O'Connor calls 'submerged population groups' (an apt phrase for the Irish in the nineteenth century and at the time of the composition of *Dubliners*); he adds 'The novel can still adhere to the classical concept of civilised society, of man as an animal who lives in a community, as in Jane Austen and Trollope it obviously does; but the short story remains by its very nature remote from the community—romantic, individualistic, and intransigent.'* From an aesthetic point of view, it seems that Irish

*Frank O'Connor: *The Lonely Voice*, Bantam Books, New York, 1968, p. 21.

writers feel more at ease in the 'face to face' relationship entailed by the narrator's role in short pieces, and in the less elaborate type of structure involved. A contemporary Irish short-story writer, Mary Lavin, has remarked that short stories 'imposed a selectivity that I might not otherwise have been strong enough to impose upon my often feverish, overfertile imagination.'* Joyce may very well have felt the same thing at the beginning of his career. Seen in that light, *Dubliners* can then be considered as a form of training—and an insufficient one at that, in view of his later achievements in which he could never master a type of construction both traditional and complex. *A Portrait of the Artist as a Young Man* is traditional but not structurally complex: it follows the linear development of the *Bildungsroman* (a novel concerned with a person's formative years and development). *Ulysses* and *Finnegans Wake* are complex, but do not adopt the structure of fiction: *Ulysses* resorts to the epic method of the *Odyssey* to support its weight of words and its awesome length; *Finnegans Wake* is based on hieroglyphs and symbolic patterns.

Irish story-tellers before Joyce, who have played their part in creating the modern form that he was to mould in his turn, may be mentioned briefly, as their work may point to different developments. Thus the so-called 'fantastic' authors, such as Joseph Sheridan Le Fanu (1814–73), Fitzjames O'Brien (1828–62) or Bram Stoker (1847–1912) lead to modern terror and science fiction; the folklorists proper lead to the works of Oscar Wilde (1856–1900) and James Stephens (?1882–1950). William Carleton (1798–1869), in such collections as *Traits and Stories of the Irish Peasantry* (1830–33), *Tales of Ireland* (1834), *The Fawn of Springvale and Other Stories* (1841) or *Tales and Sketches* (1845), proved the outstanding intermediary between the old order and the new. He preserved the legendary and popular vein but also originated the realistic trend that was to dominate with his successors—in subject, observation, and rendering of manners and of speech.

The lesson was taken up soon afterwards by the Irish cousins Edith Somerville (1858–1949) and Martin Ross (1862–1915) who collaborated on such stories as *Some Experiences of an Irish R.M.* (1899) and *Further Experiences of an Irish R.M.* (1908). Like Carleton they used rural material; they were as sensitive to laughter as to tears; and they showed the same gift for rendering linguistic particularities. Their background, however, was aristocratic—in a society where aristocracy was doomed—and their world much narrower than Carleton's. Yet they made up for such deficiencies by the breadth of their culture, their knowledge of the French and English tradition; and they herald Joyce by the coherent internal structure of each story and the careful overall structure of each collection, involving a common framework, a common

*Mary Lavin: Preface to *Selected Stories*, New York, 1959.

protagonist—for example, Major Yeates as the Irish R.M. (Resident Magistrate)—and variations on a theme that ultimately reveals its unity of purpose and design.

Finally, there is George Moore (1852–1933), a scrupulous and sophisticated writer, whose work embraces a wider outside world that he alternately loves and chastises—a dialectical attitude which places him at the fountainhead of the modern Irish tendency to express the disenchantment of individuals with a narrow, gossipy, banal, priest-ridden rural milieu, crushed by taboos and numb to feelings of beauty and pleasure.

Many of these traits are also to be found in Joyce's *Dubliners*. But there are evident differences. Moore stated in his preface to *Celibate Lives* that he preferred 'soul cries' to adventures. Nevertheless, it is only with the work of Joyce that 'adventures' either disappear totally, or become a mere occasion for an internal vision which humanises everything—even the city of Dublin, perceived like a vast paralysed body remembering the various moments of its private and public life, while death approaches.

Thus, out of a time-honoured tradition, *Dubliners* establishes a new lineage.

From country to city

Joyce has another claim to novelty in the Irish short story tradition, in his choice of material. In *Dubliners*, practically for the first time, the setting and environment become totally urban instead of rural. Even George Moore, in spite of a few incursions into the Dublin of the 1880s, remained essentially rural: the title of his main collection of stories, *The Untilled Field* (1903), is proof enough of this, although the word 'untilled' indicates a departure from the usual treatment of the subject: a wish no longer to idealise country life but to denounce its lack of culture and its parochialism.

As regards attitudes towards the country, we may wonder whether Moore was not more radical than Joyce: it is probably easier for one who comes from, or lives in, the country to be anti-rural. A townsman always has qualms on the subject. Joyce is divided, as can easily be shown by contrasting two passages from *A Portrait of the Artist as a Young Man*, quoted by two critics who have recently tackled the problem, each in order to establish the opposite thesis.

The first of these critics is Maurice Harmon, who writes that 'The awareness of the peasant world emerges in James Joyce's *Portrait of the Artist* as a deprivation.'* He continues, introducing the first passage: 'To

*'Aspects of the Peasantry in Anglo-Irish Literature from 1800 to 1916', *Studia Hibernica*, XV, 1975, p. 105.

Stephen Daedalus the peasants are attractive, holy and mysterious.' He listens with particular fascination to Davin's story of that strange encounter with the peasant woman in the Ballyhoura Hills:

> The last words of Davin's story sang in his memory and the figure of the woman in the story stood forth, reflected in other figures of the peasant women whom he had seen standing in the doorways at Clane as the college cars drove by, as a type of her race and his own, a bat-like soul waking to the consciousness of itself in darkness and secrecy and loneliness and through the eyes and voice and gesture of a woman without guile, calling the stranger to her bed.

The second critic is Terence Brown for whom 'James Joyce feared contact with the Irish soil', as seen in the following extract from Stephen's journal:

> John Alphonsus Mulrennan has just returned from the west of Ireland ... He told us he met an old man there in a mountain cabin. Old man had red eyes and short pipe. Old man spoke Irish. Mulrennan spoke Irish. Then old man and Mulrennan spoke English. Mulrennan spoke to him about universe and stars. Old man sat, listened, smoked, spat. Then said: – Ah, there must be terrible queer creatures at the latter end of the world. I fear him. I fear his red-rimmed horny eyes. It is with him I must struggle all through this night till day come, till he or I lie dead, gripping him by the sinewy throat till ... till what? Till he yield to me? No. I mean no harm.*

Needless to say, neither passage expresses Joyce's standpoint exclusively. His vision is a double one, faced as he is with the same dialectics as Gabriel in 'The Dead'; he is hostile to the West of Ireland and yet fascinated and, to a point, regenerated by it.

Divided as a townsman, Joyce is also divided as an Irishman who must choose between modernism on the one hand, primitivism and a return to the Gaelic sources on the other. And no Irishman can completely deny the latter, even though he may scoff at the Celtic Revival and its myths—a bifurcated attitude not unlike that which Joyce experienced concerning the Roman Catholic Church. Remember Stephen's answer in *A Portrait of the Artist as a Young Man*, when asked whether he intends to become a Protestant: 'I said that I had lost the faith, ... but not that I had lost self-respect. What kind of liberation would that be to forsake an absurdity which is logical and coherent, and to embrace one which is illogical and incoherent.'

On an intellectual level, however, Joyce had more respect for Catholicism than for the promotors of the Celtic Revival of the late

*'Dublin in Twentieth-century Writing: Metaphor and Subject', *Irish University Review* VIII, 1, Spring 1978, pp.9, 10.

nineteenth and early twentieth century—W. B. Yeats (1865–1939) and his followers. It is perhaps more unconsciously (with the exception of 'The Dead') that his own remote peasant origins, or Nora's less remote ones, induce some hesitation or reveal an influence: it is not unthinkable, for instance, that his extraordinary minuteness as far as topography is concerned may be rooted in his ancestors' care for their small plots of ground, carefully fenced off from their neighbours; not to mention the fact that Dublin in general (and Joyce's Dublin in particular) retains a village atmosphere.

On the surface, at any rate, Joyce is definitely a townsman and an urban writer—the first in Ireland. There are good reasons why his country should have waited so long: the main impulse that drove people towards towns in the eighteenth century—the Industrial Revolution—was practically unknown in Ireland. There are also good reasons why authors should have shifted their interest at precisely the moment when Joyce was conceiving *Dubliners*: the movement had then begun that was to empty the countryside, to concentrate more than a quarter of the population of the South of Ireland in Dublin, its capital city, and more than a third of the population of Northern Ireland in its capital, Belfast, which was also becoming the subject of short stories and novels written by authors such as Patrick MacGill (1891–1963) and Shan Bullock (1865–1935). In Dublin, Sean O'Casey (1880–1964), Flann O'Brien (one of the pen names of Brian O'Nolan, 1911–66), and Samuel Beckett (b. 1906) stand out; and among lesser novelists Paul Smith (b. 1920), Christy Brown (b. 1932), Lee Dunne (b. 1934), Brian Cleeve (b. 1921), are worthy of mention; the list is by no means complete.

Joyce was indeed a pioneer: but he was a prophet only in parts. If the main theme of *Dubliners* is paralysis and the impossibility of getting out, (which a character such as Eveline, 'passive, like a helpless animal' experiences) we may wonder whether, soon after, it was not Belfast that best answered the description; and if, nowadays, Dublin—and Belfast—are different in that respect from the rest of the world. They may still be cases of hemiplegia. But then, so are the other great cities: no island is left, anywhere.

Joyce's own Irishness

One thing is sure: even if Joyce managed to get out of Dublin bodily and to look at it from a certain geographical distance, he did not succeed in getting Dublin out of his thoughts. He wrote to Georg Goyert, on 19 October 1927, 'The book does not describe the way THEY are in Dublin, but the way WE are.' It is not even that he does not *succeed* in getting out of Dublin: he does not *want* to—as can be seen from the conversations he had at a later period with Arthur Power, who quotes him, in his book *From an Old Waterford House*, as saying 'You must write what is in your blood and not what is in your brain.' And when Power announced that he wanted to be international like all great writers, Joyce replied, 'They were national first, and it was the intensity of their own nationalism which made them international in the end.' He added—and this is a very useful statement for our study of *Dubliners*—that for himself, he always wrote about Dublin 'because, if I can get to the heart of Dublin, I can get to the heart of all the cities in the world. In the particular is contained the universal.' It is highly ironical that the last sentence should echo a similar one by W. B. Yeats: 'The grass-blade carries the universe upon its point' since Joyce, even though he admired the poet, had no great reverence for his efforts as leader of a new school of Anglo-Irish literature. This had been clear enough when he attacked the Irish Literary Theatre in *The Day of the Rabblement* and it also transpires in several sections of *Dubliners*, in 'The Sisters' for instance, if we are to believe Donald T. Torchiana's interpretation:

> The opening story . . . pictures a boy's fate, his likely future defeat as a priest of the imagination, something like the fate of Father Flynn, a genuine and no less scrupulous priest. Misunderstood by his sisters and the boy's aunt, condemned by the uncle and Mr Cotter, the priest in his relationship to the boy serves as an ironic parallel to the figure of Father Christian Rosencrux, Yeats's symbol for the imagination dormant for two hundred years in both his essay 'The Body of the Father Christian Rosencrux' and the later poem, 'The Mountain Tomb'. Yeats frequently went on to speculate that his imaginative rekindling in literature would soon break out in Ireland, the hoped-for effulgence of the Irish Literary Revival. I hold Joyce's first story to be a strong demurrer against such a possibility in the Dublin of 1895 and after.*

It also occurs in 'A Little Cloud' where A.E.'s (George Russell, 1867–1935) *New Songs* of 1904 are the butt of Joyce's satire; and in 'A Mother', particularly when we remember that one of the allegorical representations of Ireland is a certain Kathleen ni (the daughter of) Houlihan, portrayed by Yeats in a play of that title. The heroine of Joyce's story is called Kathleen, and one of the male characters (whose daughter she is *not*) is called Holohan . . .

In September 1932, Yeats asked Joyce in very amiable terms to be one of the founding members of the new Irish Academy of Letters: 'Of course the first name that seemed essential both to Shaw and myself was your own, indeed you might say of yourself as Dante said: "If I stay who goes, if I go who stays?".' These were kind words, to which Joyce replied:

*'James Joyce's Method in *Dubliners*' in P. Rafroidi and T. Brown (eds.): *The Irish Short Story*, Colin Smythe, Gerrards Cross, 1979, p. 128.

'I see no reason why my name should have arisen at all in connection with such an academy.' There *was* every reason. The criterion retained by Yeats was 'to have done creative work with Ireland as a subject matter'. Leaving aside Joyce's creativity, the Irish material is there all right!

Dubliners, faithful to its title, had no other subject than the capital of Ireland and its inhabitants, as soon would be the case with *A Portrait of the Artist as a Young Man* and *Ulysses*—which was originally designed as one of the stories in *Dubliners*; thus certain figures of the earlier volume appear in the later one as well: Doran in 'The Boarding House', for instance, is in *Ulysses* 'The lowest blackguard in Dublin when under the influence' (of drink), a proof that his forced marriage has not succeeded too well; while the guest-house in Hardwicke Street is there again; or Kernan ('Grace') whom Bloom, the main character in *Ulysses*, describes as 'that drunken little barrelly man that bit his tongue off falling down the mens W.C. drunk in some place or other'. 'Grace', in fact, is the closest link between the two books, both in tone and because several other names reappear: those of Martin Cunningham and Long John Fanning as well as M'Coy—the latter a first sketch of Bloom himself.

The Irishness of *Dubliners* can be studied on at least five levels: religious, cultural, political, geographical, and autobiographical.

Religion: The point is particularly obvious. Whether we take the entire first story, 'The Sisters', the educational background of 'An Encounter'; Ste Marguerite Marie Alacoque presiding over the destinies of 'Eveline'; the respectability and religious practice of the mother in 'The Boarding House'; 'Grace', which offers evidence of a vast knowledge of religion in general and the worldliness for which the Jesuits were reproved; or 'The Dead' with its evocation of Cistercian monks who sleep in their coffins— everything points to a type of upbringing and to a specific mood whose Irishness need not be stressed. The obsessive recurrence of religious references is particularly striking in one who is supposed to have abandoned the faith of his fathers. 'It is a curious thing,' Cranly tells Stephen in *A Portrait of the Artist as a Young Man*, 'how your mind is supersaturated with the religion in which you say you disbelieve.'

Culture: Religion intervenes not only in allusions but also among the deeper symbols. Irish culture may also be present in *Dubliners* in more or less hidden layers. Thus certain critics think that such and such a story is the modern transposition of one of the rich episodes in the cycles of the Gaelic saga, that 'The Dead' is a version of 'The Destruction of Da Derga's Hostel' or that 'After the Race' is a new rendering of 'Nial of the Nine Hostages and his Son Laoghaire'. Others have suggested that some of the pieces in *Dubliners* are images of the history of the country: 'An Encounter', for instance, in which, to quote from Donald T. Torchiana's essay, 'time and again, we happen on places of historical encounters where the Irish ultimately lost, however apparent the victory might have seemed'; or 'After the Race' which presents a kind of summing up of the destiny of Ireland that was about to be saved by the French and was all the better fettered to the English ...

Such hypotheses are not absolutely convincing, however, and it may be wiser simply to notice the number of references to Irish architecture, music and literature; to Celtic literature in general (for example, the allusions to the Tristan and Isolde story in 'A Painful Case'); to Anglo-Irish literature in, for example, 'Ivy Day', the remarkable pastiche of patriotic ballads produced in the previous decades in newspapers and collections such as *The Spirit of the Nation* (1843). See also the use made of Thomas Moore's Irish melody, 'The Song of Fionnula'—'Silent, O Moyle, be the roar of thy waters'—in 'Two Gallants'.

Politics: Politics bring us back to 'Ivy Day in the Committee Room' with its description of Dublin's political ways and with the figure—also an obsessive one—of Ireland's 'uncrowned king', Charles Stewart Parnell (1846–91), whose messianic role was cut short by British hypocrisy and Irish puritanism playing in alliance, and who was betrayed by his own followers when it was discovered that he had an attachment to a married woman. Parnell, the subject of Joyce's first published work, *Et Tu, Healy* is to be found again in *A Portrait of the Artist as a Young Man*, in the quarrel between Mrs Dante and Stephen's father on Christmas Day; in four of the chapters of *Ulysses* (Aeolus, Hades, Oxen, Eumaeus); and throughout *Finnegans Wake*, where he is one of the manifestations of the phoenix.

Geography: References to places are too numerous to be detailed here. Joyce's father used to say of his son: 'If that fellow was dropped in the middle of the Sahara, he'd sit, be God, and make a map of it.' He did, indeed, map out Dublin, not only in *Ulysses* but in *Dubliners* as well.

Autobiography: Even in the first three 'childhood' stories which are the most autobiographical, what we have is a fictional Joyce, which is stressed by the fact that his young heroes (contrary to his own real background) always appear as orphans, with no brothers or sisters, living with their uncles and aunts. In the following pieces, what we get, at best, is a projection of Joyce's fears of what he might have become, had he stayed in Dublin.

All the same, something of Joyce's own Irish life creeps into nearly every story (his own life, as in 'Araby' or 'An Encounter', or his brother's, as in 'Ivy Day'). Many a character had a counterpart in reality: his father, friends, acquaintances—some well known, like Oliver

St John Gogarty (1878–1957), who is the Gallaher of 'A Little Cloud'.

Sometimes there even is autobiography in a deeper sense, revealing personal tendencies such as his love-hate relationship with money, his fondness for the bottle, and his jealousy. The episode of Gretta's first love in 'The Dead' is, for instance, the accurate transcription of a happening in the early life of Nora Joyce—who once went out with a young man suffering from consumption, Michael Bodkin, whose end was hastened by his coming to say farewell to her on a cold night, the eve of her departure from the west of Ireland.

That cardinal point is an apt conclusion of our bird's eye view of Joyce's Irishness: it was in the West of Ireland, where Joyce went in pilgrimage on one occasion, that he chose his life companion—not some intellectual high-brow, but a plain, nearly rustic, girl; as if he was obeying the primitivistic injunctions of a follower of the 'Celtic Twilight'.

The struggle for publication

Two more texts by James Joyce may help us to grasp the two reasons, one aesthetic, the other visceral, as it were, that explain the contradictions we have been faced with, as well as the hazards and misfortunes encountered in the publication of *Dubliners*. The first of these texts is part of a letter Joyce wrote to his brother Stanislaus on 20 November 1906, in which he describes his reactions at reading a collection by Seamus O'Kelly called *By The Stream of Killmeen* (1906). Of the characters—'beautiful, pure faithful Connacht (*) girls and lithe, broad-shouldered, open-faced young Connacht men'—he remarks:

> Well, there's no doubt they are very romantic young people; at first they come as a relief, then they tire. Maybe, begod, people like that are to be found by the stream of Killmeen, only none of them has ever come under my observation as the deceased gent in Norway remarked.

The second one is also taken from a letter to the same correspondent but was written earlier (September 1905). It proclaims: 'Give me for Christ sake a pen and ink-bottle and some peace of mind and then, by the crucified Jaysus, if I don't sharpen that little pen and dip it into fermented ink and write tiny little sentences about the people who betrayed me, send me to hell.'

What appears in the first passage is a rejection of romanticism and idealisation in the name of realism or naturalism, an aesthetic choice

*Ireland is divided into four provinces: Ulster in the north with Belfast as its capital, Leinster in the East with Dublin as capital, Munster in the South with Cork as capital and Connacht (or Connaught) in the West with Galway as capital.

corroborated in a letter to Grant Richards dated 5 May 1906: 'He is a very bold man who dares to alter in presentment, still more to deform, whatever he has seen and heard.' There is no denying that realistic streak in a man so concerned with detail that he could say of himself: 'I have a grocer's assistant's mind', though it would be a mistake to view Joyce as a kind of literary photographer: he was conscious of a need to transcend immediate data. He wrote to his brother: 'Don't you think there is a certain resemblance between the mystery of the mass and what I am trying ... to give people some kind of intellectual pleasure or spiritual enjoyment by converting the bread of everyday life into something that has a permanent artistic life of its own ... for their mental, moral, and spiritual uplift.' But at the time he was writing *Dubliners*, and the first part of the process was probably the more important, for motives which the second passage quoted at the beginning of this section explains: not only did he refuse, on behalf of a certain aesthetic creed, to idealise reality the way romanticism does; but, out of a desire for retaliation, he wanted to lay stress on its ugly and seamy sides, to have a 'special odour of corruption' float over his stories (the remark is in the same letter to Richards, 5 May 1906). Little did George Russell (A.E.) know what he was in for when he started Joyce on *Dubliners*, asking him for something 'simple, rural, live-making, pathos [pathetic]' ...

The history of the publication of Joyce's collection of stories is closely linked with the two attitudes just mentioned. On the one hand, it was expected of an Irish writer of the Revival period that he should resemble someone like Seamus O'Kelly. On the other hand it is equally certain that Joyce's spirit of vengeance and derision—however subdued it may appear in *Dubliners*—could only shock those who were in favour of some form of graceful Celtic melancholy.

It was the printer who objected first. On receiving 'Two Gallants'—a late addition, in which several points made him raise an eyebrow—he started re-reading the lot and denouncing here an allusion, there a situation or a phrase; Joyce, in spite of all his vigorous protests, had, for instance, to expunge six uses of 'bloody'.

In these cases a question of so-called 'morality' was involved. With his next publisher, Richards, who finally burnt the manuscript (luckily there were several copies), what appeared objectionable was the treatment of Edward VII in 'Ivy Day'. Joyce, stubborn as only Irishmen can be, went to the length of writing to his successor at Buckingham Palace in order to check whether he actually felt offended. He received this answer from the secretary: 'It is inconsistent with rule for His Majesty to express his opinion in such cases.' Joyce then announced his plight publicly in the columns of *Sinn Fein*, 2 September 1911. All was in vain. But Richards was to accept and publish *Dubliners* only three years later, and there is evidence that he relented not out of conviction but simply because a certain notoriety was beginning to attach itself to the young man whose *A Portrait of the Artist as a Young Man* had been accepted by *The Egoist*.

A last irony was that the book made little noise and created no scandal, very much what Joyce's character Little Chandler had expected for himself: 'He would never be popular: he saw that. He could not sway the crowd, but he might appeal to a little circle of kindred minds.'

A note on the text

The stories in *Dubliners* may be arranged—according to the author's indications—into four categories, as follows:

(a) STORIES OF CHILDHOOD 'The Sisters'; 'An Encounter'; 'Araby'

(b) STORIES OF ADOLESCENCE: 'Eveline'; 'After the Race'; 'Two Gallants' *(added later)*; 'The Boarding House'

(c) STORIES OF MATURE LIFE: 'A Little Cloud' *(added later)*; 'Counterparts' *(both concerned with married life)*; 'Clay' *(concerned with a spinster's life)*; 'A Painful Case' *(concerned with a bachelor's)*

(d) STORIES OF PUBLIC LIFE: 'Ivy Day in the Committee Room' *(political)*; 'A Mother' *(cultural)*; 'Grace' *(religious)*.

It is not quite clear whether the fifteenth story should be added here or, preferably, considered as a fifth section by itself, devoted no longer to the life of Dublin and Dubliners but, as the title 'The Dead' implies, to their death and, perhaps, their resurrection.

The date and first place of publication of each story are indicated in Part 2 of these Notes. The stories were first published in book form by Grant Richards, London, in 1914. The edition used for these Notes is the Triad Panther paperback edition published by Granada, 1977.

In the quotations from *Dubliners* in these Notes, all words in italic type (except *was*, p. 39, *artiste*, p. 44, *Secreto*, p. 50, and *your*, p. 88) have been italicised by the present author and are not so printed in the original text.

Part 2

Summaries*
of DUBLINERS

Stories of childhood

The Sisters

PUBLICATION: 13 August, 1904, in *The Irish Homestead*, A.E.'s newspaper, under the pseudonym of Stephen Daedalus.

SETTING: The narrator's home, where he lives with his uncle and aunt; Great Britain Street, Dublin, where an old priest has just died at his sisters' place.

CHARACTERS: The two main characters are the boy-narrator and the dead priest, the Reverend James Flynn, formerly of St Catherine's Church. Around the boy appear his uncle and aunt as well as a friend of theirs: old Cotter, a 'tiresome old fool'. The priest's two spinster-sisters are Eliza and Nannie. Another priest, Father O'Rourke, is mentioned several times but is not seen.

PLOT: A boy has been befriended by a sixty-five-year-old priest living in retirement. He has been expecting his death for a long time, but now the priest has experienced a third stroke and is paralysed, and the boy knows death is imminent. He goes past the priest's place once more and back at home he hears from old Cotter, obviously hostile to his relationship with Father Flynn, that death has occurred. The boy does not betray any feeling but experiences a very vivid dream of the priest — to whose house he returns in the morning, although he has not the courage to enter. But his aunt takes him there in the evening. He then sees his old friend in his coffin and listens to his elders' conversation, which gradually builds up a picture of total failure utterly different from what the boy had imagined.

SIGNIFICANCE: Autobiographical elements: in the child, Joyce probably makes use of himself in print for the first time; in the uncle, he makes use of his father; Flynn was the name of his mother's grandfather, and on this side of the family there had been a priest who became harmlessly insane and lost his parish.
    This is the first setting of the general theme of paralysis (see the very

*I wish to thank Christine Huguet, Edith Linglart, and Anne-Marie Moreau whose work and discussions have helped me with parts of this section.

first sentence in the story) and also of the motif of death which links 'The Sisters' with the last story of the collection. It is a study in appearance and reality (notice the contrast between the priest lying in state and what we hear of his life, or between the 'big discoloured teeth' and the boy's romantic dream of Persia—to be taken up again in 'Araby'; beauty is of the imagination, ugliness of reality). It is a study in human ambiguity: the boy is sad that the priest has died and yet feels as if he 'had been freed from something by his death'; the priest is considered a failure and yet has widely contributed to opening the boy's mind to knowledge. Such fundamental complexities are rendered through an equal complexity of structure (study the relationship of the dream, which is broken into several parts) and viewpoint (the priest's character is revealed through the testimony of different witnesses, through dream as well as reality).

'The Sisters' hints at the incapacity of the Church (represented by the broken chalice) to help man to a balanced, creative, un-paralytic life; yet the permanent fascination of religious rites retains its grip. There is a possible symbolic implication that the priest stands for the *Irish* Catholic Church which sells vocations to susceptible children (young James long wanted to become a Jesuit)—hence the use of the word 'simony'—and insists on being served while failing the people that serve it. In this light, Eliza's remark 'God knows we done all we could, as poor as we are . . .' would make her and her sister representatives of those Irish people whose language they certainly use.

NOTES AND GLOSSARY:

gnomon: in geometry (Euclid) part of a parallelogram which remains after a similar parallelogram is taken away from one of its corners

simony: traffic in sacred things (from the name of Simon Magnus who offered money to Christ's Apostles for the gift of conferring the Holy Ghost)

catechism: the book giving the elements of the Christian religion, in the form of questions and answers

stirabout: Anglo-Irish for 'porridge'

he had a great wish for him: 'great esteem' (*Irish, meas mór*) not 'great desire'. No ambiguity in the priest's feelings is indicated here; 'The Sisters' is not 'An Encounter'

beady: beadlike, small, round and glittering eyes

to box his corner: hold his own in any fight

Rosicrucian: strictly, a member of a secret order founded in 1459 by Christian Rosenkreutz; Rosicrucians claimed various forms of magic knowledge. Used here in the loose sense of 'dreamer'

nipper: *(slang)* boy, lad

simoniac: an adept at simony

R.I.P. *(Requiescat in Pace)*: *(Latin)* 'May he rest in peace', a formula of the Roman Catholic Church whose official language was Latin until the Vatican Council of 1965 which authorised the use of the vernacular. In Joyce's time all religious services were in Latin, while the Protestants had been using English since the Reformation

at check: arrested

High Toast: a brand of snuff

The Irish College in Rome: after the Penal Laws of the seventeenth century, Irish candidates to the priesthood had to study abroad, seminaries being forbidden in Ireland till the foundation of Maynooth in the late eighteenth century. There were Irish colleges in Louvain, Lille, Douai, Paris, Rome, and elsewhere, some of which still remain

sins mortal or venial: the Catholic catechism made a distinction between serious ('mortal') transgressions, that deprived people of the state of grace and led them to perdition if they died unabsolved, and minor ones ('venial'). Absolution could only be given by a priest in confession. The priest could not reveal what he had heard (hence, the later allusion to 'the secrecy of the confessional')

confessional: the box in which the priest hears confessions

chalice: the cup used in the celebration of the Eucharist or Mass

we crossed ourselves: Catholics make the sign of the cross (forehead, breast, shoulders) in memory of Christ's death, and to proclaim their faith

in state: placed in view with due ceremony

cream crackers: dry biscuits

did he ... peacefully?: 'Did he *die* peacefully', an ellipsis for the sake of euphemism (that is, saying less, in order not to shock)

a Tuesday: Irish use for 'on Tuesday'

anointed: administered the sacrament of extreme unction. This sacrament for dying people includes the applying of consecrated oil (anointment)

such a beautiful corpse: notice Joyce's humour even at unexpected moments

we done: for this and other instances of Irish popular syntax, see section on 'Texture' in Part 3

The Freeman's General: illiterate rendering of the *Freeman's Journal*, a Dublin nationalist newspaper

breviary: the book containing the 'Divine Office' for each day, which priests were bound to recite

Irishtown: a poor quarter of Dublin between Ringsend and Sandymount

new-fangled: new fashioned; a reference to the appearance of pneumatic tyres

rheumatic: a malapropism for 'pneumatic' (malapropisms are named after Mrs Malaprop in the comedy *The Rivals* (1775) by Richard Brinsley Sheridan (1751–1816))

crossed: thwarted, unhappy (compare Shakespeare's 'star-crossed lovers'; but also an obvious pun on Father Flynn's profession)

It contained nothing: either there was no wine in it, or the wine had not yet been trans-substantiated into the blood of Christ as it is at consecration during the Catholic Mass

---

An Encounter

PUBLICATION: 1914. Written in 1905, published in the first edition 1914.

SETTING: *(a)* school *(b)* route of adventure: from north-east to south-east of Dublin: Canal Bridge, North Strand Road, Vitriol Works, Wharf Road, Smoothing Iron, then across the river Liffey on a ferry-boat, Ringsend in the direction of the Pigeon House and back.

TIME: A mild sunny morning in the first week of June; noon on the quays; afternoon in a field across the river.

CHARACTERS: (In order of mention or appearance): Joe Dillon, a fierce boy with a vocation; Leo Dillon, his fat young brother, an idler, too timorous to play truant; Father Butler (modelled on the Rector of Belvedere College, Father William Henry); Mahony, the boy who goes in for games while the unnamed narrator, also a young boy, is more of a bookworm; the man with the stick and the jerry hat.

PLOT: The narrator and his friends regularly meet to 'arrange Indian battles'. He, however, gets bored with the monotony of these games and the routine of school-life. He delights in reading 'Wild West' stories and American thrillers. He yearns for 'real adventures' and 'wild sensations'. So, one day, Mahony and the narrator decide to miss school and go to the Pigeon House. They cross the river Liffey and spend some time watching a ship and her crew. When they arrive at Ringsend, they find it is too late to reach their destination. They sit in a field. A man passes them, then retraces his steps, sits beside them and starts a conversation. He first dwells on school, books and 'sweethearts', stressing that 'every boy has a little sweetheart' and that there is 'nothing he likes so much as looking at a nice young girl, at her nice white hands and her beautiful soft hair'. At this point, the narrator senses there is something peculiar about the man. The stranger then goes away for a few minutes and presumably masturbates, although we can only guess since the narrator (out of refusal or consent?) ignores what is going on and Mahony merely exclaims: 'I say! Look what he's doing!' When he comes back, Mahoney gets up to chase a cat. The man resumes his monologue, contradicting this time his previous statements, asserting 'if ever he found a boy talking to girls, he would whip him and whip him.' From then on, he keeps explaining how pleasurable it would be to 'whip such a boy'. The narrator, frightened, walks away, trying to look calm and undisturbed, but his voice betrays fear when he calls his friend.

STRUCTURE: There are three parts to the story: (1) The spirit of adventure enters school-life; (2) The expedition; (3) The actual encounter of the strange man who comes to the boys three times.

SIGNIFICANCE:
(a) Autobiographical basis: James had actually played truant from Belvedere with his brother Stanislaus and, on their way along the strand to the Pigeon House, they had met a homosexual.
(b) A study in psychological oppositions. Notice Mahony's un-complicated, straightforward, extrovert nature, with a solid grasp on the outside world and a knowledge of what he is after (for instance, 'have some gas with the birds') and the introspective, introvert narrator with a touch of snobbery, a superiority complex and a habit of living in a world of clichés and passivity when confronted with 'sin'.
(c) A tale of initiation where the hero goes forth to seek adventures, becomes more and more isolated, finds temptation, terror and instruction. Or rather, a tale of false and incomplete initiation (he runs away). Notice also the gap between the type òf adventures sought and what actually occurs.
(d) Symbols have been found profusely, particularly concerning the sort of quest the boys are engaged in: they headed for the 'Pigeon House', possibly an allusion to the Holy Ghost whose traditional emblem is the dove, a Spirit that the Catholic Church seems to have lost—'what would Father Butler be doing out at the Pigeon House?' The trouble is that the House in question, once the terminus of the Irish-English packet service, then used as a fort, a lighthouse and a power station, is so-called simply because it was built by John Pigeon! They only encounter a pervert, (but what does that pervert stand for? Ireland? He has green

eyes. A surrogate of God? Note the insistence on the number three, which might suggest the Trinity, throughout the story: three-part structure, three magazines mentioned, a 'three-master', 'three o'clock', 'three totties', and the possible allusion to the Bible at the beginning: 'The summer holidays were near at hand' — 'The kingdom of God is nigh at hand' (Luke 21:31) and at the end of the story: 'And I was penitent; for in my heart I had always despised him a little' — 'And she despised him in her heart' (2 Samuel 6:16) or 'A man shall be commended according to his wisdom: but he that is of a perverse heart shall be despised' (Proverbs 12:8). Death? See the section on 'Semantics' (p.67) for Donald T. Torchiana's historical interpretation and B. Ghiselin's view that the story tells of the defeat of the theological virtue of hope.

LANGUAGE AND STYLE: The viewpoint is a schoolboy's, hence the instances of childish humour (for instance: 'Leo Dillon was afraid we might meet Father Butler or someone out of the college; but Mahoney asked, *very sensibly*, what would Father Butler be doing out at the Pigeon House. *We were reassured.*') and the frequent use of slang. The story is one of sexual initiation built up by sensuous words (for instance, 'The granite stone of the bridge was beginning to be *warm*, and I began to *pat* it with my hands in time to an air in my head. I was very happy', and 'what he wanted was to get a nice *warm* whipping'). It is also a study in corruption matched by some notations of squalor and seediness.

NOTES AND GLOSSARY:

Wild West:	far west of the United States, the scene of cowboys' and Indians' fights as recounted in 'westerns'
The Union Jack, etc.:	popular magazines of the 1890s
unkempt:	uncombed, dishevelled, untidy, rough; just the opposite of what proper girls should be
Apache:	a red Indian tribe
National School:	an ordinary local free school, not a first class 'college' like Belvedere. Notice the snobbery of Father Butler
consciences:	remorse
miching:	dialectal for playing truant, missing school
mates:	*(slang)* boys, companions
coping:	uppermost part of stone or brickwork
pipeclayed:	whitened with paste
Mall:	Charleville Mall (walk), along the Royal Canal in Dublin
gas:	*(slang)* fun
Bunsen burner:	a gas burner, used in scientific laboratories, named after R. W. Bunsen. It consists of a metal tube with an adjustable air valve at the base

funk:	*(slang)* flinch from it, panic
bob:	*(slang)* a shilling (there were twenty in the pre-metric pound sterling)
tanner:	*(slang)* sixpence (half a shilling)
ragged:	probably a reference to the 'Ragged Schools' in Dublin which catered for the children of the very poor
Swaddlers:	a nickname for Protestants invented by a Catholic, ignorant of the Bible, who heard a Methodist preacher refer to the infant Christ 'wrapped in swaddling clothes'
Smoothing Iron:	an entrance to a bathing place, shaped in that form. It has disappeared since Joyce's time
how many:	how many strokes of the cane
skit:	*(slang)* fun
huckster:	a small shopkeeper
Dodder:	a river rising in the Dublin mountains and flowing into the River Liffey at Ringsend
provisions:	food, but a pun may have been intended, the original meaning of the word (*Latin:* 'providere', to foresee) hinting at the fact that the boys' expected vision (the Pigeon House) has crumbled
Jerry hat:	a round felt hat. Short for 'Jeremy' (many people in the trade were Jews)
Thomas Moore:	a famous nineteenth-century Irish poet (1779–1852), author of the *Irish Melodies*
Walter Scott:	Sir Walter Scott (1771–1832), poet, antiquarian and father of the historical novel
Lord Lytton:	Edward Bulwer, first Baron Lytton (1803–73), also an historical novelist, author of *The Last Days of Pompeii* (1834)
totties:	*(slang)* girls (derived from Hottentot)
josser:	fellow, but also, sometimes, a priest

Araby

PUBLICATION: 1914. Written in 1905 (completed by mid-October).

SETTING: North Richmond Street where the narrator lives, the station down Buckingham Street (Amiens Street, now Connolly Station), the train to Westland Row Station (now Pearse) and the bazaar ('Araby in Dublin', Grand Oriental Fête), which was actually held 14–19 May 1894 in aid of Jervis Street Hospital.

CHARACTERS: The ghost of a previous tenant, a priest; the narrator; his uncle and aunt; Mangan's sister; a visitor: Mrs Mercer ('an old, garrulous woman, a pawnbroker's widow, who collected stamps for some pious purpose'); a young lady with an English accent in charge of one of the stalls of the bazaar. But perhaps the bazaar itself should be mentioned among the characters and North Richmond Street, which is personified: 'blind', 'quiet', with houses 'conscious of decent lives within them', gazing at one another 'with brown imperturbable faces'.

PLOT: The narrator is in love with the sister of one of his mates, Mangan. They never speak to each other until one evening she mentions to him that she would like to go to the Araby bazaar, but won't be able to go on account of a retreat that week in her convent. He promises to go and bring her something. He then lives in expectation of the event, daydreaming of her to the extent that he doesn't work well at school any more. On the great day, Saturday, he waits for his uncle to come home from the pub and give him the florin necessary for his trip. The uncle arrives late. The boy does not reach the bazaar until ten minutes to ten when everything is closed or closing. He has no time to choose a gift for his beloved and has to leave in sadnesss and anger.

STRUCTURE: (1) from 'Every morning I lay on the floor' to 'my body was like a harp and her words and gestures were like fingers running upon the wires': the dawning of love. (2) from 'One evening I went into the back drawing-room' to 'ugly monotonous child's play': first rendezvous and wait. (3) Saturday: last wait and disillusion.

TIME: Evening, with the exception of the beginning of part (3).

THEMES AND STYLE:
(a) Autobiography: same unnamed narrator as in the first two stories, with same love for books and adventure, same propensity for dreaming, same family background — he lives with his uncle and aunt; setting used in 'The Sisters' for the place where the priest died, now identified as a house in North Richmond Street, where the Joyces actually lived at number 17; Joycean theme of the young artist carrying his chalice among a crowd of foes, to be taken up again in *Stephen Hero*.
(b) Theme of illusion (oriental dreams, easy love) and reality (shabbiness of surroundings, in street and bazaar alike, hence the number of words and phrases such as 'musty', 'waste-room', 'littered with old useless papers', pages of books 'curled and damp' and 'yellow', 'wild' garden, 'straggling bushes', 'rusty bicycle-pump', 'brown, sombre' houses, 'feeble lanterns', 'dark muddy lane'; the 'high, cold, empty, gloomy rooms'; the 'ruinous houses'; the inanity of the conversation in the market; the pervading references to money into which all splendour resolves, transforming eastern marvels into mere 'wares', in contrast with the amorous epiphany during which the narrator's heart 'leaps', his

eyes feed on Mangan's sister's figure, dress, and intimation of underclothes ('petticoat') and his whole body is 'like a harp'.

(c) Theme of first unrequited love, sexual and sentimental awakening: 'My eyes were often full of tears (I could not tell why) and at times a flood from my heart seemed to pour itself out into my bosom.' By the way, is not the description a bit too heavy for Joyce to be quite serious here?

OTHER LEVELS OF SIGNIFICANCE: Should one go further and follow, for instance, Ben L. Collins's suggestions* that the central apple tree in the yard likens it to the Garden of Eden from which Adam was cast into the world of reality for having listened to the serpent, represented here by the rusty bicycle pump now inoperative (it cannot inflate, that is, raise and elate any more); or that the heroine stands, among other things, for Ireland, since she is called 'Mangan', the name of a famous Irish poet James Clarence Mangan (1803–49), the author of 'Dark Rosaleen' (an allegory of his country)?

NOTES AND GLOSSARY:

Christian Brothers: a teaching order

The Abbot: Scott's novel, published in 1820, a sequel to *The Monastery*, in which appear Mary Queen of Scots and Roland Avenel, a romantic youth

The Devout Communicant: a religious tract written by Pacificus Baker, a Franciscan friar (1813)

The Memoirs of Vidocq: Vidocq was a French criminal who became head of the Police. The *Memoirs* were translated into English in the very year of their publication in France (1828) by the Irishman William Maginn (1794–1842)

come-all-you: a type of ballad starting with these words

O'Donovan Rossa: a Fenian nationalist leader (1831–1915) sentenced to penal servitude in 1865

retreat: a period of retirement from ordinary occupations for devotion to religious exercises

Freemason: members of that secret society were excommunicated by the Catholic Church

The Arab's Farewell to his Steed: a poem by Mrs Caroline Norton (1808–1877), the grand-daughter of Sheridan and the supposed original of George Meredith's (1828–1909) *Diana of the Crossways* (1885). The opening lines are: 'My beautiful, my beautiful! that standest meekly by,/With thy proudly arched and glossy neck, and dark and fiery eye'.

*In *Twentieth Century Interpretations of 'Dubliners'*, ed. Peter K. Garrett, Prentice Hall, Englewood Cliffs, N.J., 1968, pp.93 ff.

Café Chantant:	*(French)* singing pub, or public house, a place where drink is sold and consumed
salver:	a tray
fib:	*(slang)* lie

Stories of adolescence

Eveline

PUBLICATION: In *The Irish Homestead*, 10 September 1904.

SETTING: The front room of a 'little brown house' in Dublin with a view on the street; the station at the North Wall.

CHARACTERS: Only two actually appear: the 'heroine' (if she may be called so), Eveline, a nineteen-year-old girl, the eldest child of a large family, and a shop assistant; her friend, Frank, a sailor fond of music and story-telling. But Eveline's parents are vividly evoked: her dead mother, her violent father, as well as some of the people related to her past, brothers or playmates; and to her present, like Miss Gavan, her boss in the shop.

STRUCTURE AND PLOT: There are three main parts: exposition, illumination, (failed) action. In the first part, we learn of Eveline's past and present life, a hard one, on account of the poverty, the work (she not only has to earn a living, she must look after her father and the two younger children), the drunkenness and brutality of her parent. We also hear of her young man Frank, who has asked her to leave with him for Buenos Aires, presumably as his wife. Still, Eveline hesitates to escape, out of a sense of duty, out of fear of an adventurous future, her present life being difficult but not 'wholly undesirable'.

The sound of a street organ changes the course of Eveline's reflections. On the one hand it reminds her of her promise to her mother 'to keep the house together as long as she could' (an organ had played the same tune as she lay dying); on the other hand it kindles her revolt against 'that life of commonplace sacrifices closing in final craziness'. Her decision is taken: she will be saved and live. She is ready to elope with Frank.

Once at the station, however, she feels completely paralysed and cannot follow him.

POINTS OF INTEREST AND SIGNIFICANCE: In the overall structure of *Dubliners*, this is the first story of the sequence devoted to adolescence where Joyce balances two feminine polarities: virgin and temptress in what is, by and large, a man's world. Eveline representing the woman-victim, her treatment is probably more sympathetic, although it is difficult to decide whether pity or irony dominates (some critics have read 'Eveline' like the pastiche of a romance). Perhaps, in any case, Joyce is too 'clinical' to intimate anything more than the notion of failure. Escape and elopement fail except for the very strong (and Eveline lacks fortitude). Nor can the 'good' life (if such a thing exists) be sought in 'high' society ('After the Race'), venality ('Two Gallants') or lust ('The Boarding House').

To come back to the notion of fortitude it should be noted, however, that if the lack of such quality plays no minor part in Eveline's predicament (dreams and reminiscences do not help to build a future, nor penny romances; innocence can be synonomous with stupidity, and the same is true of uncritical attachment to moral or religious values)— nowhere more than in this study of the paralysis of action does Joyce lay so much stress on the smothering influence of environment, social and economic conditions. Hence the choice of certain words and the repetition of certain phrases: evening invading the avenue, odour of dusty cretonne (twice), tired, dead, broken, evening deepening, close, dark room, melancholy air, nausea, drown, passive, helpless—as well as insistence on the force of habit among those who have not the means of shaking it off (what for?), by the use of negatives or semi-negatives of resignation ('they *seemed* to have been *rather* happy then. Her father was *not so bad* then. She did *not* find it a wholly *un*desirable life.') and of the question marks of hesitation ('Was that wise?').

This first story of adolescence, and one in which the main character, a girl, is no longer Joyce himself, shows a definite shifting of the point of view. The third person is used (instead of the first) and two voices at least can be heard: the narrator's (now detached and observant, now the omniscient creator, although he intervenes as unobtrusively as possible); and Eveline's, whose inner monologue we are given.

NOTES AND GLOSSARY:

to keep nix: to serve as a lookout

harmonium: a kind of parlour organ operated with bellows pumped by pedals

Blessed Margaret Mary Alacoque: the term 'Blessed' is used in the Catholic Church for such candidates to canonisation as have not yet been proclaimed 'saints' by the Pope. Margaret Mary Alacoque has become one since. She was a French nun (1647–90) who, in her convent of Paray-le-Monial, had several visions of the Sacred Heart

Melbourne: capital of the state of Victoria, Australia

stores: large department shops, in Joyce's days the equivalent of supermarkets in ours

The Bohemian Girl: an opera (1843) by the Irish composer Michael Balfe (1808–70). The libretto by Alfred Bunn was based on a story by Cervantes

Straits of Magellan, Patagonia: South America

Buenos Aires: the capital of Argentina

Howth: a well-known hill, residential area and pleasure resort on Dublin Bay. The village of Howth is on the northern side of it

Derevaun Seraun: probably a garbled version of a Gaelic phrase meaning 'farewell to the white oak-woods'

After the Race

PUBLICATION: In *The Irish Homestead*, 17 December 1904.

SETTING: Dublin in summer (the car race referred to was actually run on 2 July 1903, for the Gordon-Bennett International Automobile Racing Cup, in the conditions and with the results indicated by Joyce). As the story opens the young men are motoring back from the finish line to central Dublin via the Naas Road, up Inchicore, down Dame Street, past the Bank of Ireland, through Grafton Street. After dinner, they stroll along Stephen's Green and make for Westland Row Station where they board an eastbound train to Kingstown (now Dun Laoghaire). Once near the sea, they get into a rowboat and assemble on a yacht for supper, music and cards. The story begins in late afternoon and ends on the yacht at daybreak.

CHARACTERS: Jimmy Doyle, a twenty-six-year-old Irishman, the son of a wealthy butcher, educated at Trinity College and Cambridge, a snob who wants to be seen with the international set of motorists and their friends, and whose vanity (in spite of solid instincts) will make him lose.

The so-called international set:

Charles Ségouin, the owner of the car, 'well worth knowing', as Jimmy's Father says, because of his immense wealth and his fame in motoring circles.

André Rivière, Charles's cousin, a young electrician of Canadian birth.

Villona, a huge Hungarian, a brilliant pianist, a refined conversationalist and an optimist by nature, in spite of his poverty.

Routh, a torpid Englishman obviously lacking in culture but not in an ability to win at cards.

Farley, a young American, the owner of a yacht.

Jimmy's father, the astute butcher, also appears briefly.

STRUCTURE AND PLOT: A three-part scene structure interspersed with two transitional interludes, each scene building up to a climax immediately followed by an anti-climax.

Scene 1: Motoring back from the race. *Climax:* 'Rapid motion through space elates one; so does notoriety; so does the possession of money' (a beautiful example of three-beat rhythm) to: 'the journey laid a magical finger on the genuine pulse of life and gallantly the machinery of human nerves strove to answer the bounding courses of the swift blue animal'—an apt metaphor to bring the epiphany to a close. *Anti-climax:* 'They walked northward with a curious feeling of disappointment in the exercise, while the city hung its pale globes of light above them in a *haze* of summer *evening*.'

Interlude 1. Jimmy's house, where the young Irishman and Villona go to change and meet Mr Doyle.

Scene 2: Dinner at Ségouin's hotel. *Climax:* throughout (see the first words: 'The dinner was excellent, exquisite'). *Anti-climax:* the conversation grows spiteful. Ségouin 'threw open a window significantly. That *night* the city wore the *mask* of a capital.'

Interlude 2. Trip to Kingstown.

Scene 3: Supper, music, cards on *The Belle of Newport*. *Climax:* throughout (first exclamation: 'It is beautiful!'). Note all the other exclamations: 'What merriment!', What good company they were!', 'What excitement!'. *Anti-climax:* intimated at the beginning of the last paragraph by the world 'morning' in: 'He knew that he would regret it in the morning', achieved through Villona's announcement: *'Daybreak, gentlemen!'* while 'standing in a shaft of *grey* light'.

POINTS OF INTEREST AND SIGNIFICANCE: This is one of Joyce's most interesting stories from the point of view of structure.

Tone: there is no pity on the author's part as in 'Eveline'. The mood has become satirical and will remain so for the rest of the collection, with the possible exception of part of 'Clay', 'A Painful Case' and 'The Dead' (each time, on account of a female character—even though Joyce can also satirise women, as, for instance, in the case of the mother in 'The Boarding House' and in 'A Mother').

Social and economic criticism of the poor (in 'Eveline') is extended to the provincial and cosmopolitan rich in the present story. The former set is denounced for their heaviness, lack of real daring ('reasonable recklessness'—a fine example of oxymoron), vanity, snobbery, longing 'to see life' (about which their view is nonsensical) and ultimate silliness, since they become the easy preys of strangers to whose enterprises they deliver Ireland, that 'channel of poverty and inaction', no match for the foreigners' 'wealth and industry'. The latter set is denounced not only for their lack of scruples but for their artificiality (note such words as 'hilarious', 'light', 'volubly and with little reserve', 'flashing', 'excited'). Political criticism is added: of the nation's general attitude (e.g. 'the gratefully oppressed'), of Irishmen's cliché-visions of themselves and their relationship with the sister-island (obtuse and pitiless though she is: for instance Routh is completely at sea when he is told about English madrigals, but wins the money in the end). Notice in this respect the sentence ending on a critical comment of Joyce's highly reminiscent of Mr Crofton's last pronouncement in 'Ivy Day': 'Jimmy, whose imagination was kindling, conceived the lively youth of the Frenchman twined elegantly upon the firm framework of the Englishman's manner. A graceful image of his, he thought, and a just one.' Joyce also makes fun of the pseudo-revolutionary spirit which people give up as soon as they have enough money to turn conservative ('His [Jimmy's] father, who had begun life as an advanced Nationalist, had modified his views early') and whose main usefulness is to start a fight after too much drink (see the end of scene 2).

The preceding remarks cover surer ground than the allegorical interpretations of some critics, for instance those of Zack Bowen and Donald T. Torchiana, or even more so the latter's equation of 'After the Race' with the Gaelic story of Niall of the Nine Hostages and his son Laoghaire. Here is Bowen's comment:

> Young Doyle finally comes to understand that the last 'great' game lies between Routh and Ségouin, as history repeats itself in the struggle between France and England. Jimmy, Ireland, as in the days of Tone [Theobald Wolfe Tone, 1763–98, who tried to free his country from the British yoke with the help of the French], having been an unimportant but involved bystander in the struggle, understands that 'he would lose, of course'. As Routh and England emerge triumphant, Farley and Jimmy, the fat, wealthy American and the Irishman with aspirations are the heaviest losers.'*

Torchiana has this to say:

> No less drastic historically appears the likely necessity of defeat, when, as in 'After the Race', an Irishman gains the allegiance of the French in any contest with the English. The sense of triumph that flushes the faces of James Doyle while riding in a winning French car after the 1903 Gordon-Bennett Cup Race sharply recalls Irish enthusiasm after another such famous race won by the French. I speak of course of the famous Races of Castlebar, the jibing appellation affixed to the British rout by a small French and Irish force

*Zack Bowen, article in *James Joyce's 'Dubliners'*, ed. Clive Hart, Faber & Faber, London, 1969, p.173.

under General Humbert in 1798 after the landing at Killala. But it's the aftermath, as Joyce's title suggests, that must preoccupy us. In the story, aboard the yacht in Kingstown harbour, the Englishman Routh wins the final game of cards over the Frenchman Ségouin. But the heaviest losers are the Irish-American Farley and the Irishman Jimmy Doyle. Just so after the Races of Castlebar. A second engagement lasted but a half hour when the French surrendered. Their officers and men were well treated, even feted in Dublin. The Irish were massacred on the spot and their officers summarily executed. 'Our friends the French', the traditional slogan said to link patriotically Catholic France to Catholic Ireland in their joint enmity for England, turns out to be inevitably disappointing, perhaps even collusive in Ireland's usual defeat.*

And from the same source:

Just as pertinent, though more muted as befits legend, is Joyce's use of Dun Laoghaire in 'After the Race', at the time called Kingstown. To contemplate Doyle senior, the former butcher and merchant prince, and his son Jimmy is also to glance at the continuing fates of Niall of the Nine Hostages and his son Laoghaire. Niall had embraced the hag Royal Rule to get the kingship at Tara; he had sought to advance himself on the Continent; one story has it that he was slain by a British arrow shot by a rival backed by the Franks. Laoghaire was known for his attention to Irish law, his formulating the Senchus Mor, and then for resisting the Boromean Tribute—cattle, sheep, and swine—due King Tuathal of Leinster. Captured during that resistance, he swore by the four elements never to repeat his refusal. However, he broke his oath and was immediately struck down by them. In the face of this legendary account, the flickering ironies in the fortunes of the Doyles, whose money and position are dependent upon meat, need not be drawn out. Yet the father is a kind of prince collaborating with royal rule; despite his patriotism, police contracts had allowed him to expand his business. He is also a parent who has sent his son to college and then to Cambridge in England. The son in turn has lost him a good deal of money to a Briton while in the company of Frenchmen in whose enterprise the father had encouraged the son to invest, thus hoping to extend both their social lives into Continental circles. Jimmy had dabbled in law at Trinity and now has returned to the family stronghold, formerly Dun Laoghaire, after a foray near Naas, once King Tuathal's base in exacting the Tribute. Breathless and excited, Jimmy is struck by the dawn's light on a body of water, Dun Laoghaire/Kingstown Harbor, where, disarmed, relieved of his

*Donald T. Torchiana, article in *The Irish Short Story*, ed. P. Rafroidi and T. Brown, Colin Smythe, Gerrards Cross, 1979, p.133.

money, slumped toward earth, his head in his hands, he must nevertheless face his friends, the French.

NOTES AND GLOSSARY:

scudding: racing

Gallicism: not the usual sense of 'French idiom', but 'French mode of being'

Dublin University: Trinity College, the Protestant university set up in 1591, a place few Catholics attended in Joyce's time (he himself went to the rival institution, University College) unless they belonged to the Establishment or, like Jimmy Doyle, wanted to make friends with its members

a term to Cambridge: three months in one of England's two oldest universities (the other is Oxford) was also something only a wealthy Irishman could afford

mite: a small contribution

Cadet Roussel: a famous French song about a volunteer of 1792 named Rousselle (Joyce's spelling is wrong) and who had everything by threes (for example, three houses). The refrain is: *'Ho! Ho! Hohé, vraiment!/Cadet Rousselle est bon enfant'*

I.O.U's: 'I owe you', a document to acknowledge a debt

Two Gallants

PUBLICATION: 'Two Gallants' was written in 1906, a late addition to the original plan, and started Joyce's trouble with the printer. It was first published with the rest of the collection in 1914.

SETTING: The time is a Sunday evening, grey and warm, in August. From the topographical point of view this is one of Joyce's most detailed stories, from the triumphant walk of the two young men down the hill of Rutland Square to their late encounter at the corner of Ely Place, via Trinity College, Nassau Street, Kildare Street, Stephen's Green, Hume Street (where they part), Grafton Street, Rutland Square, Capel Street, Dame Street, George's Street, back to Grafton Street, Merrion Street, Baggot Street and the Green again, a circular walk. Nor are these spots the only ones mentioned; one of the characters refers to Dorset Street where he spent the afternoon talking in a pub, the other to the distant South Circular Road where he used to pick up girls and he takes his present conquest to Donnybrook, a suburb once famous for its fair, dating from the time of King John.

CHARACTERS: If we leave out one or two friends of Lenehan's with whom he holds a brief and uninteresting conversation, and Corley's girl who is seen (and whose attire and figure are even described in detail) but not heard, the two 'gallants' are the only characters of note in the story. They are both revealed through appearance, gait and conversation—inner monologue intervening also, but solely for Lenehan, the only one to remain throughout on the stage. There is also a harpist, but mention is only made of his fingers and his eyes, and the harp appears more of a persona than her (note Joyce's personification) player.

PLOT AND STRUCTURE: Two friends, Corley and Lenehan, are walking together, busy talking about the girl-friend Corley is about to meet. Lenehan wonders whether Corley will manage to obtain from her something that remains unnamed but seems very important to him, but Corley claims he knows how to take women. The friends separate. Corley goes away to Donnybrook with the girl and Lenehan resumes his wandering. He feels old, lonely and dejected and he whiles away the time first inside a cheap restaurant then along the streets, until he reaches the meeting point at the appointed time. The couple finally turn up and Lenehan follows them unnoticed. Corley walks the girl home, she enters, comes back and gives Corley something. He starts away, Lenehan having to run on his heels and get nearly angry before his friend reveals the results of his efforts: 'A small gold coin shone in the palm' [of his hand].

Structurally, 'Two Gallants' is different from the rest of the stories with its four parts, its *coup de théâtre* at the end of parts 1 and 4, its general mystery and suspense:

(1) Presentation and general conversation of the two men ending, on the completely unexpected—and, to the reader, incomprehensible—question: 'Well ... tell me, Corley, I suppose you'll be able to pull it off all right, eh?'
(2) Continuation of the conversation and the walk (during which they meet a harpist) till the girl appears: '" There she is," said Corley.'
(3) The men have parted, Corley going his way, Lenehan another. Lenehan's solitary walk, inner monologue and more and more impatient waiting.
(4) 'Suddenly he saw them coming towards him'—to the revelation, in the very last sentence, of what it was Lenehan expected Corley to wheedle out of his girl-friend, or rather the half-revelation, for how was that money earned and for what purpose?

INTEREST AND SIGNIFICANCE: This is probably one of the most difficult stories to interpret in *Dubliners*. One of the 'adolescence' group, Joyce tells us, although here (with the characters in their early thirties) and even more so in the next piece, the term has to be strained extensively (or is prolonged adolescence, the refusal to grow old, another form of paralysis?). An illustration of the sin of covetousness—but not very convincing from that point of view.

It is obviously an instance of literary pastiche; notice in the very first paragraph, the insistence on warm grey evening', the number of heavy words of romance origin ('descended', 'circulated', 'shuttered for repose', 'illumined'), continued later with 'rotundity'.

It is literary satire, then, but attacking what school or tendency? Probably Irish romantic and post-romantic poetry and thought, a vain striving after an impossible purity, and a resultant pining away in melancholy—like Fionnuala, the daughter of Lir (a Celtic deity) whose plight (she was turned into a swan and condemned to wander for centuries) is sung in Thomas Moore's 'Irish Melody' played by the harpist in this story. This is seen as an evasion of the reality—Irishmen betraying their own country for money, instead of fighting against the economic exploitation of Ireland by England and her helpers. In that light, Donald T. Torchiana is right to call our attention to the fact that the harpist is playing 'not far from the club' and to comment:

> Unobtrusively Joyce has placed the key to the interlocking scenes of the story into our hands. For, instead of aimless wanderings through Dublin that the story seems at the best to afford, we recognise a landscape some two hundred years old. The club is the Kildare Street Club, bastion of a declining Ascendancy, and an off-shoot from the older Daly's Club, where half the land of Ireland was said to pass through the gambling hands of a sporting nobility and gentry. In Corley (Lord Corley in *Ulysses*) and Lenehan we get the Garrison remnant of those former Ascendancy Bucks, still doing in Ireland and getting paid for it to boot. As Joyce once said of British rule, and its instrument the Ascendancy in Ireland, 'She enkindled its factions and took over its treasury'. Consequently, every place name in the story speaks of that Williamite and Georgian period and its profitable betrayal of Ireland's interest. From Rutland Square to the Shelbourne Hotel to Hume Street, the half-sovereignty, exposed in the small gold coin at the end, merely attests to that formula.*

Equally right are the many other critics who have identified the servant girl, with her 'frank rude health' and 'unabashed blue eyes', with Ireland, Kathleen-ni-Houlihan turned half-prostitute.

Other literary allusions in the text point to a pastiche of romantic fiction. Thus 'Lothario' is not only the heartless libertine in Nicholas Rowe's (1674–1718) *The Fair Penitent* (1703) but a character in the German writer Goethe's (1749–1832) *Wilhelm Meister* (1829), while the very title, 'Two Gallants'—as appears in a letter Joyce wrote to Grant

*See *The Irish Short Story*, ed. P. Rafroidi and T. Brown, Colin Smythe, Gerrards Cross, 1979, p.129–30.

Richards on 5 May 1906—was a jibe at the French writer Alexandre Dumas's (1803–70) idea of gallantry.

Should we search for other symbolical significances? Let's content ourselves with pointing out that religious and liturgical references have been found (particularly to the Last supper on account of phrases like 'That takes the biscuit!') by such critics as Florence L. Walzl.*

NOTES AND GLOSSARY:

takes the biscuit:	*(slang)* is the best I have ever heard
recherché:	*(French)* rare. The conjunction of the sophisticated French word and the familiar 'biscuit' is particularly incongruous
leech:	a blood-sucking worm, hence one who sticks to other people to suck gain out of them
round:	of drinks: buying everyone a drink
limericks:	a form of Irish nonsense verse, generally with licentious undertones
tissues:	tip sheets or racing forms
tart:	*(slang)* girl of dubious reputation
slavey:	*(slang)* servant
cheese:	*(slang)* the real thing
in the family way:	pregnant
up to the dodge:	*(slang)* knows how to avoid becoming pregnant
Pim's:	a large and highly-respected Quaker general store
hairy:	*(slang)* clever, astute
about town:	in the round of social functions, fashionable
pull it off:	succeed
game:	spirited enough
Lothario:	see 'Interest and Significance' above
mug:	*(slang)* a stupid person
Ditto:	the same
on the turf:	*(slang)* she has become a prostitute
Ecod:	a mild oath
Silent, O Moyle:	the first line of 'The Song of Fionnuala', one of the *Irish Melodies* (II, 9, 1825) by Thomas Moore (1779–1852). The first verse runs: 'Silent, O Moyle, be the roar of thy water,/Break not, ye breezes, your chain of repose,/While, murmuring mournfully, Lir's lonely daughter/Tells to the night-star her tale of woes/When shall the swan, her death-note singing,/Sleep, with wings in darkness furl'd?/When will heaven, its sweet bell ringing,/Call my spirit from this stormy world?'

curates: Anglo-Irish slang for bartenders
a little of the ready: a little money, wealth
Egan's: a pub

The Boarding House

PUBLICATION: Composed in Trieste in 1905 at the same time as 'Counterparts', in torrid weather. 'Many of the frigidities of "The Boarding House" and "Counterparts"', Joyce was to remark, 'were written while the sweat streamed down my face on to the handkerchief which protected my collar'. In the early scheme for the book, this was the first story about adolescence. When preparing it for publication, Joyce made it the last, probably on account of the age of the main character (thirty-four or thirty-five) and of the introduction of marriage (both little Chandler and Farrington, in the first two stories of mature life, are married). It first appeared in 1914 with the rest of the collection.

SETTING: A circumscribed part of Dublin: Spring Gardens are mentioned at the beginning since Mooney's butcher's shop was there, but the rest of the story takes place in the boarding house Mrs Mooney runs in Hardwicke Street, from which can be heard the bells of St George's (Protestant) church, and which is within walking distance of the Catholic cathedral in Marlborough Street. As the title implies, everything here takes place indoors (in contrast with 'Two Gallants') and the description is rather minute (breakfast-room, drawing-room, stairs, bedrooms), giving an impression of shabby gentility.

CHARACTERS: The Mooney family: father (not seen, but referred to several times), a good-for-nothing, a drunkard, once a butcher's foreman who married his employer's daughter, now a more or less unemployed sheriff's man, utterly disreputable; mother, 'The Madam' of the boarding house she has established after separating from her husband, an astute, awe-inspiring matron; son, Jack Mooney of the 'thick bulldog face' with 'a pair of thick short arms', a violent sort of character with bourgeois pretentions in spite of his vulgarity; daughter, Polly (like the heroine of Gay's *The Beggar's Opera*, also, partly, a story about marriage) 'a slim girl of nineteen', with 'light soft hair and a small full mouth', 'eyes ... grey with a shade of green', and the looks of 'a little perverse madonna'.

Apart from other lodgers vaguely mentioned in the background and the maid, Mary, we then have the man who is caught in the Mooneys' trap: Mr Doran, a thirty-four or thirty-five-year-old bachelor, slightly higher on the social scale (he finds Polly a little vulgar and knows she will be looked down upon by his family), with his wild oats (mostly) behind him—a clerk or executive in a wine-merchant's office, altogether eligible on account of his seriousness, respectability and salary ('he had a bit of stuff put by' as Mrs Mooney remarks).

PLOT AND STRUCTURE:
(a) Flashback: presentation of the Mooney family and setting of the trap: how to oblige a young man (still unnamed) to marry Polly.
(b) Immediate past and present: Mrs Mooney's preparation for the decisive battle on a bright Sunday morning: her daughter has confessed the loss of her 'virtue', which her mother has contrived, as they both know but never suggest; she is about to confront the young man whose name we learn at last.
(c) Immediate past, and present, a quarter of an hour later than beginning of *(b)*: Doran's predicament: he has been to confession the night before and told he owes the girl 'reparation', and now Polly comes to tell him of her own avowal to her mother. Flashback: he remembers how it all happened. Then he is asked to go and see the Madam in the parlour. He obeys the summons and on his way down passes Polly's brother, Jack, whose attitude clearly tells him that should Doran fail to set matters right, Jack will 'bloody well put his teeth down his throat'.
*(d)*Present: Polly waits for the dénouement which is announced in Mrs Mooney's voice: 'Come down, dear. Mr Doran wants to speak to you', and underlined with a last ironical sentence of the author's.

INTEREST AND SIGNIFICANCE: This is a straightforward story, although, possibly because the boarding house in Hardwicke Street connects with the 'boardelhouse' in the same street mentioned in *Ulysses* (where Doran is also referred to), some critics have made a Ulyssean reading of it. Thus, Richard Levin and Charles Shattuck in 'First Flight to Ithaca'* consider that 'The Boarding House' is told within an Homeric framework, Polly being Aphrodite, the goddess of beauty; Doran being Ares, the god of war (he has a red beard like the god); Mrs Mooney, Hephaestus (Aphrodite's lame blacksmith husband who builds a net to catch them); Jack Mooney (who works in Fleet Street) Poseidon, the god of the sea—a possible interpretation even if the change of sex required for Mrs Mooney (whose feminine nature is hardly questionable) may make readers other than American academics slightly uncomfortable. Nathan Halper—also an American—suggests† that Doran (the name in Gaelic means an 'exile' or 'stranger') is Odysseus; Polly, Nausicaa the daughter of King Alcinoos who befriends Odysseus; and then, as she is about to get married, Penelope, the faithful wife of Odysseus who waits in Ithaca for his long-drawn-out return from Troy; hence the waiting at the end.

*In S. Givens (ed.): *James Joyce: Two Decades of Criticism*, Vanguard Press, New York, 1948.
†In Clive Hart (ed.): *James Joyce's Dubliners*, Faber & Faber, London, 1969, p.81.

There may also be symbolical or other significances attached to some of the proper names of persons or places: Polly and Doran have already been mentioned, as well as Fleet Street. It is perhaps no coincidence that the street chosen for the setting of the story should be named after one of the Lords Hardwicke, since a 1751 Act regulating marriage contracts is called Hardwicke's Act. Did also Joyce introduce St George's Church ironically to compare the fight of St George killing the dragon and the victory of Mrs Mooney over Doran? Is a character named Sheridan to hint at the possible scandal (although 'scandal' means 'slander' in Richard Brinsley Sheridan's play *The School for Scandal*)?

By and large, however, the interest of 'The Boarding House' lies elsewhere. It lies in the variety of the points of view (see 'Plot and Structure' above); in the fact that it is one of Joyce's most 'naturalistic' stories (particularly in the descriptions of the various parts of the house, the portraits, the half-disgusted references to food, as in 'A Painful Case', with the 'yellow streaks of eggs with morsels of bacon-fat and bacon-mud', 'the crusts and pieces of broken bread' that 'help to make Tuesday's bread-pudding'), the accumulation of details tending to show how the main character is literally trapped by the combined forces of social conventions and moral taboos. Notice in this respect the importance of the adverb, in 'he was sitting *helplessly*' which was the very word used for Eveline and brings up the theme of paralysis again, but linked this time with the impossible coexistence of 'instinct' (the word occurs four lines before 'helplessly' and is repeated) and community rules, especially if the community is not a big one. (Notice, 'Dublin is such a small city: everyone knows everyone else's business'.) Many words are taken from the realm of military life but the battle is lost beforehand: instinctive lust— the normal sexual urge—cannot be satisfied outside marriage, and married life is doomed to failure.

Thus the link with the next story (although one of 'mature' life) becomes evident, as is evident Joyce's own stand as regards 'the joys of connubial bliss' ('A Little Cloud'). He may, as a matter of fact, have been thinking of Nora—with whom he lived but refused to marry for a great many years—when drawing the portrait of Polly. Nora served in a hotel which was hardly more than a boarding house when he first met her, 'she *was* a little vulgar', but James certainly did not despise her and does not seem to have regretted what he calls his 'delirium' in a striking euphemistic ellipsis (those were not days when the so-called 'act of love' could be described at length, and the indirect references of the earlier paragraph—'the first casual caresses', the 'loose open combing-jacket', the 'white instep', the 'perfumed skin'—were already daring enough for the time). Joyce denounces neither sex nor women but the institution of marriage, which is equated with a mere money bargain.

Other highlights of this essentially *satirical* piece are the denunciations of hypocrisy (see the interview between mother and daughter) and the role played by priests (see, for instance, 'she went to the priest and got a separation from him, with care of the children'; and see also Doran's confession: 'the priest had drawn out every ridiculous detail of the affair, and in the end had so magnified his sin that he was almost thankful at being afforded a loophole of reparation'). 'The Boarding House' is, with 'Grace', the most anticlerical story of someone who vanquished paralysis by refusing the common Irish pattern illustrated by Doran: free-thinking in youth and a 'regular' life in maturity.

NOTES AND GLOSSARY:

pledge:	in Ireland, as in other countries where alcoholism is a problem, people can join teetotallers' associations by pledging (swearing) they will never drink again
cleaver:	a butcher's chopping knife
artistes:	the French word is used throughout to add a fashionable and exotic touch and because the English equivalent is more limited
chummy:	friendly
small hours:	of the morning, that is, very late
mits:	*(slang)* hands
vamped:	improvised
run:	the opportunity of meeting and catching one of the young men by looking after (as well as for) them
volumes:	prayer-books
short twelve:	Low Mass (which is shorter than High Mass) at twelve o'clock
brunt:	violent attack
screw:	*(slang)* salary
stuff:	*(slang)* money
pier-glass:	tall mirror
Reynolds Newspaper:	an Irish radical weekly founded in 1850
breast:	'to make a clean breast', to confess
combing jacket:	a sort of bathrobe or dressing gown
Bass:	a particular brand of beer

Stories of mature life

A Little Cloud

PUBLICATION: Written in 1906, first published with the rest of the collection; this was one of Joyce's favourites.

SETTING: The little cloud is no part of the physical setting but probably refers to the gleam of hope—or epiphany—that comes into the main character's life in the course of the story, where he is first seen at his desk in the King's Inns (lawyers' offices), then along Henrietta Street, Capel Street and Grattan Bridge towards Corless's bar, a fashionable place in the centre of Dublin, and finally in his home, probably somewhere in the suburbs. In the Bible (1 *Kings*, 18:44), after a long drought sent by Jehovah as a punishment, Elijah's servant had joyfully reported to his master: 'there ariseth a little cloud out of the sea, like a man's hand'.

CHARACTERS AND PLOT: This is a story with the usual tripartite construction. The first part reveals the mind of Little Chandler, a shy, fragile and unsuccessful clerk with literary pretensions, as he anticipates his meeting with Ignatius Gallaher, an old friend of his and now a famous London journalist on a visit to 'dear, dirty Dublin'. The second section covers the actual meeting, during which Gallaher keeps showing off and patronising the little man and Chandler gets more and more confused, unsatisfied and ... tipsy. The last part shows Little Chandler back at home where he ponders upon his relationship with his wife and the general mediocrity of his life. Then, after a flight into poetry, he takes out his fury on his infant son who has disturbed him. He is scolded by Annie (his wife) on her return and sinks into helpless remorse.

STRUCTURE: The point of view follows the divisions mentioned above: everything is seen through Little Chandler's eyes in sections 1 and 3; part 2 is presented from the outside by the author-narrator. The method used is one of contrasts, flashbacks and flashforwards. Among the latter, note, for instance, how the main character's reaction to his child at the end is forecast by the apparently gratuitous paragraph: 'A horde of grimy children populated the street. They ... *crawled up* ... or squatted like *mice* upon the thresholds. Little Chandler *gave them no thought*. He picked his way deftly through all that minute *vermin*-like life ...' Contrasts are to be found at several levels: psychological (the striking difference between Chandler and Gallaher is conveyed by means of narrative style and dialogue): thematic (contrasts between imagination and reality: Gallaher seen as 'unspoiled' at the beginning of the story; the use of escapist poetry in counterpoint to real life).

OTHER POINTS OF INTEREST AND SIGNIFICANCE:
(a) Autobiographical basis: there seems no reason to assume that Little Chandler is Joyce—although he may be a picture of what he thought he might have become. Ignatius Gallaher, on the other hand, had his counterpart in real life: Fred Gallaher, a newspaper man who, because of some scandal, had to leave for London and Paris. Joyce has him in mind

here (as he has in *Ulysses*), and has probably added touches borrowed from Oliver St John Gogarty's personality—he was to write to his brother on the occasion of Gogarty's marriage: 'Long health to Ignatius Gallaher!' It is also likely that Joyce drew on his own experience for his description of children and 'the joys of connubial bliss'.

(b) Importance of the theme of marriage in this first story of 'mature life'. Stanislaus Joyce went as far as to state* that 'A Little Cloud' ought to be read as 'nothing more' than a simple story about matrimony, 'with the figure of a successful and impenitent bachelor in it to cause discord and cast a little cloud over married life' (in which case, the title comes to mean the very reverse of what we suggested in the paragraph devoted to the 'setting'—but Joyce liked phrases with double entendre).

(c) Literary satire of the 'Celtic note' and its wistful sadness.

(d) A study of 'envy' (see Part 3 of these Notes).

(e) A study of the paralysis not of artists in general but of certain would-be writers, whether successful—like Gallaher who remains on the surface of everything, or unsuccessful—like his friend. Little Chandler *dreams* of artistic achievements, as he does of travel and high life, but he has never done anything more than toy with the idea of creative work. He is the victim of history ('He emerged from *under* the *feudal* arch' as opposed to the old *nobility* of Dublin' that *'roistered'*); of environment ('the poor stunted houses' and the description of Chandler's own home with its 'mean' furniture); of immobility (for economic reasons he has never been any further than the Isle of Man); of marriage, and of his own temperament—a melancholy loser, too timorous and discreet to do something, finding refuge in the vicariousness of inaccessible romance (his daydreaming about 'dark Oriental eyes ... full ... of passion [and] of voluptuous longing', so different from his wife's), of escapist poetry or a wishful daydreaming enjoyment of a career he has not even started.

NOTES AND GLOSSARY:

North Wall:	the quay used by passenger ships departing from Dublin (see end of 'Eveline')
Chandler:	this is an Anglo-Irish term for 'meat maggot'. If Joyce, as is very likely, chose the name on purpose, the description of the 'minute vermin-like life' to be found on the following page takes on an extra dimension
Atalanta:	a beautiful huntress in Greek mythology, noted for her grace and agility: she was almost invincible in running and killed any suitor who could not out-distance her.

*'The Background to *Dubliners*,' *The Listener*, 51, 25 March 1954.

half-time	'slow down, take it easy'
the Celtic School:	the poets of the Irish revival in the 1890s and early twentieth century (such as W. B. Yeats)
Lithia:	a bottled mineral water
a good sit:	a good situation
the Land Commission:	an organisation which dealt with the transfer of farm lands from landlords to tenants wishing to buy them with the backing of British credit
booze:	*(slang)* drink
Moulin Rouge:	a famous Paris night-club
cocottes:	*(French slang)* prostitutes
a rum world:	a strange world
parole d'honneur:	*(French)* word of honour
a.p.:	appointment
deoc an doruis:	not 'a small whisky' in Irish as Gallaher believes in his crassness, but 'the drink of the door', a parting or farewell drink
equipoise:	balance
fling:	a spell of unrestrained indulgence of one's impulses
Bewley's:	several famous coffee shops (Bewley's Oriental Cafes) in central Dublin
on the hire system:	by instalments
Hushed are the winds:	the first stanza of Lord Byron's (1788–1824) poem 'On the Death of a Young Lady' in the poet's first collection: *Hours of Idleness* (1807). Little Chandler stops in the middle of a line: 'That clay, where once such animation beam'd.'
lambabaun:	lamb-child

Counterparts

PUBLICATION: The work was completed by 12 July 1905. First published in 1914 with the rest of the collection.

SETTING: Crosbie and Alleyne, a lawyer's office off Eustace Street; Terry Kelly's pawn shop in Fleet Street; Patrick O'Neill's pub in Henry Street; then two other pubs, The Scotch House and Mulligan's (in Poolbeg Street); after which the main character takes a tram at the corner of O'Connell Bridge and gets off at the Shelbourne Road where his home is.

CHARACTERS: The people in Farrington's office: Miss Parker; Mr Shelly; Higgins; Farrington himself (whose physical portrait is given, and whose spiritual crisis is the subject of the story); his arch-enemy, Mr Alleyne, the boss, with a piercing North of Ireland accent, 'a little man wearing gold-rimmed glasses on a clean-shaven face', his head 'so pink and hairless it seemed like a large egg'; one of Mr Alleyne's distinguished customers, Miss Delacour. Farrington's pals in the pubs: Nosey Flynn, O'Halloran, Paddy Leonard, plus 'a young fellow named Weathers who was performing at the Tivoli as an acrobat and knock-about *artiste*' and a young woman from the same Dublin theatre, although she is not Irish and speaks in a London accent. And finally Farrington's young son, Tom.

PLOT AND STRUCTURE: This is again a tripartite story. (1) Farrington, a minor clerk of lazy and thirsty disposition, is told off by his chief, revolts and has to apologise. (2) He borrows money in order to quench his thirst and tells his story, Mr Alleyne asking him the imprudent question 'do you think me an utter fool?' — 'So, I just looked at him — coolly, you know . . . taking my time you know. "I don't think that's a fair question to put to me", says I.' His success, however, is short-lived, as he loses his reputation as a strong man, having been defeated twice by Weathers on a feat of strength. (3) Back at home, Farrington revenges himself on life in general, his mediocrity, his humiliation, the fear of future persecution in the office, and his wife's absence, by striking vigorously at his young son with a walking stick.

SIGNIFICANCE: Robert Scholes remarks that '"Counterparts" offers us, in its title and its plan, a major clue to the whole structure of *Dubliners*. The title of this story suggests both the harmonious balance of counterpointed musical parts and the anonymous interchangeability of cogs in a great machine. In the story itself, Mr Alleyne bullies the shiftless Farrington and Farrington bullies the hapless Tom. The Farringtons — father and son — are counterparts as unlovely victims. But Farrington and Mr Alleyne are counterparts as abusers of authority. And beyond this story, the brutal Farrington's return to his wifeless home and whining son is the counterpart of Little Chandler's encounter with *his* tiny son. . . . Similarly, Gallaher, in 'A Little Cloud', is related to Weathers in 'Counterparts', representing an alien London world which challenges and in some sense defeats Dublin (as the Englishman Routh defeats Jimmy Doyle in 'After the Race').'*

Among possible symbolical and other interpretations are:

(a) the opposition between North (Mrs Alleyne) and South of Ireland.
(b) Farrington's counter-progress as a pilgrim.
(c) Farrington as shadow (in law, a counterpart is the opposite part of an indenture, that which is not the original).
(d) the walking stick as sexual replacement, substitute for impotence, and applied by Farrington to his son (a copy of himself).

*Clive Hart (ed.): *James Joyce's 'Dubliners'*, Faber & Faber, London, 1969, p.93.

(e) another indictment of married life. In November 1906 Joyce wrote to his brother: 'I am no friend of tyranny, as you know, but if many husbands are brutal the atmosphere in which they live (vide "Counterparts") is brutal and few wives and homes can satisfy the desire for happiness.'

There are a few allusions or phrases that were considered objectionable in the story and played a part in the refusal of the manuscript: 'a man with two establishments to keep up'; 'she brushed against his chair' (the latter passage was actually rewritten, and the girl's legs, whose position she often changed, replaced by the sight of a plump arm). These are mild enough allusions for someone whose selected letters show how much he was obsessed by sex; but the trend is present.

It appears that the final episode is taken from life. It was William Murray's child (William Murray was James Joyce's maternal uncle) who said to his father: 'I'll say a *Hail Mary* for you, pa, if you don't beat me.'

NOTES AND GLOSSARY:

tube:	a speaking tube for inter-office communication
courses:	dishes
mind:	pay attention
slake:	diminish, quench
the objective of his journey:	Farrington pretends he is going to the toilets
a 'g.p.':	a glass of porter (stout, dark brown beer)
caraway seed:	sucked to mask the smell of the drink
manikin:	midget (used contemptuously of a little man)
two establishments:	a wife and a mistress to cater for
bob:	*(slang)* shilling; twelve pence of the pre-decimal pound sterling
pawn-office:	a place where you can borrow money after leaving an object as security for the sum
dart:	scheme
crown:	a five-shilling piece
consignor:	i.e. Farrington, who consigns his watch
a half one:	a small whisky
tailors of malt:	tumblers of unblended whisky
the liberal shepherds in the eclogues:	eclogues are pastoral (shepherds') dialogues as in Virgil's works. Joyce is probably thinking of Shakespeare's *Hamlet* (Act 4, Scene vii) in which the queen refers to 'liberal [that is, free-spoken] shepherds'
nabs:	probably variant of 'nibs' *(slang)*, a mock title for someone in authority
bevelled:	changed direction, made off at an angle

ballast office: the administrative headquarters of Dublin harbour
a small Irish and Apollinaris: Irish whiskey with sparkling mineral water
the hospitality was too Irish: too generous
sponge: parasite
knack: right trick
gab: beak, snout
pony up: drink up
smaham: sip
at the chapel: at church, for evening devotions
Hail Mary: the Roman Catholic prayer to the Virgin, starting
with that salutation used by the Archangel Gabriel

Clay

PUBLICATION: 1914, with the rest of the collection. Joyce started work on the story in November 1904 and did not complete it till late in 1906. It was successively called 'Christmas Eve', 'Hallow Eve' (at that stage, Joyce tried to have it published in one of the 1905 issues of *The Irish Homestead*), 'The Clay' and 'Clay'.

SETTING: The kitchen of the 'Dublin by Lamplight' laundry at Ballsbridge (a rather elegant south-east residential area) which actually existed and was used by Joyce. The heroine then takes a tram to the Pillar (Nelson's Pillar, in the centre of Dublin; it was blown up in recent years and no longer exists) and goes shopping nearby and in Henry Street. She boards another tram going north towards Drumcondra and gets off at the Canal Bridge. The rest of the story takes place in the Donnellys' house.

CHARACTERS, STRUCTURE AND PLOT: It is impossible in this story—the shortest of the collection—to separate these elements as everything centres round Maria's personality, as saint, 'a veritable peace-maker'—a phrase which recalls Matthew's Gospel, 5:9: 'Blessed are the peace-makers: for they shall be called the children of God'; and as witch, 'Maria was a very, very small person indeed, but she had a very long nose and a very long chin' and 'Maria laughed and laughed again till the tip of her nose nearly met the tip of her chin'. This is a duality quite consistent with the double feast being celebrated: Hallowe'en (31 October), the last night of the year in the old Celtic calendar, during which the dead walked, and All Saints' Day (1 November), the Christian festival into which the pagan tradition was transformed.

The other characters, in the laundry (the matron, Ginger Mooney, Lizzie Fleming), in the shop (the stylish young assistant), in the tram (the stout elderly gentleman with a square red face and a greyish moustache), or at the Donnellys' (Mrs Donnelly, Joe, their children, the next-door girls) are there as foils to Maria and to punctuate her progress. That progress is said to have been designed in three stages in the fashion of *La Divina Commedia*, the Divine Comedy (1309–20) by the Italian poet Dante Alighieri (1265–1321): (1) *Inferno (Hell):* the laundry; (2) *Purgatorio (Purgatory):* the Dublin streets (and trams); (3) *Paradiso (Paradise):* the Donnellys'.

We do, however, get the impression that it works the other way round, as Maria's heavenly saintliness in her place of work goes wrong the moment she steps out, and even more so when she enters her friends' house where her peaceableness becomes ineffective and she meets with the omen of death (clay, the 'soft wet substance' which she first feels with her fingers while blindfolded for a game) or, at best, convent life (the prayer book) for the rest of her short life.

SIGNIFICANCE: Critics have generally insisted either on the saint (for instance, W.T. Noon: 'Joyce's "Clay": An Interpretation', *College English* XVIII, 1955, 93–5) or on the witch (for instance, R. Carpenter and D. Leary: 'The Witch Maria', *James Joyce Review*, III, 1959, 3–7). But the importance of 'Clay' may well lie elsewhere. It is, in the section devoted to 'mature life', the first study in sterility (the second being 'A Painful Case'), the sterility of humility and celibacy. Maria is in love with herself (see the mirror scene) and her state of innocence; she refuses to see the world as it is (that is, she mistakes condescension for kindness) and ignores her vital impulses, particularly sexual, her refusal and willing ignorance being conveyed through the simple-mindedness of the vision and the style (which are Maria's throughout the story) and through her laughter, blushings and omissions:

> 'Lizzie Flemming said Maria was sure to get the ring ... Maria had to laugh and say she didn't want any ring or man either.'

> 'The stylish young lady behind the counter ... asked her was it a wedding-cake she wanted to buy. That made Maria blush and smile at the young lady.'

See also where she sings the first verse of her song twice, omitting the second, consciously or otherwise, because it runs thus:

> I dreamt that suitors besought my hand,
> That knights upon bended knee,
> And with vows no maiden heart could withstand,
> That they pledged their faith to me.
> And I dreamt that one of this noble host
> Came forth my hand to claim;
> Yet I also dreamt, which charmed me most,
> That you lov'd me still the same.

Even on the night when—in Ibsen's phrase—the dead awaken, Maria is incapable of shaking off the clay on her coffin.

NOTES AND GLOSSARY:

barmbracks:	speckled buns containing currants, a special treat of Hallowe'en
dummy:	a dumb person
Whit-Monday:	a holiday, the Monday after Pentecost Sunday
Dublin by Lamplight:	the name refers to the fact that the Protestant spinsters who ran the place employed ex-prostitutes ('a Magdalen's home' Joyce says), with the exception of Maria, of course
tracts:	Protestant religious tracts
ring:	the All-Hallow Eve (31 October, Eve of all Saints or Hallowe'en) cake contains a ring. Whoever gets it is supposed to get married within the next twelve months
Mass morning:	All Saints' Day for Roman Catholics is a holiday of obligation, that is, they must attend mass before (or now, after) they go to work—at any rate in countries like Ireland where this is normally a working day, contrary to the Continental practice
two and four:	two shillings and fourpence, a considerable sum for Maria
a drop taken:	an Irishism, for 'when he has drunk a drop too much'
smart:	impertinent as well as clever. Compare with Farrington's witticism in 'Counterparts'
stout:	dark brown beer or porter, malt flavoured
saucers:	part of a game of divination. The saucers contain sundry objects (among them a prayer book) and substances (clay) which are supposed to suggest a person's fate
a soft wet substance:	the clay
I Dreamt that I Dwelt:	a song from Michael Balfe's opera, *The Bohemian Girl*, referred to in previous notes on 'Eveline' (see p.29). The composer is mentioned again in the final paragraph

A Painful Case

PUBLICATION: 1914, with the bulk of the collection. Originally entitled 'A Painful Incident', it was first written in July 1905 and revised many times.

SETTING: The whole story is a vesperal or even nocturnal one, whether it takes place in the main character's room at Chapelizod (a village west of Dublin, on the road to Maynooth and Sligo) in which black predominates, with only an odd touch of white and scarlet (or purple); or in Central Dublin where Mr Duffy works in Baggot Street, eats in George's Street and attends an occasional concert at the Rotunda or in Earlsfort Terrace. Nocturnal also are his visits to the lady's cottage 'outside Dublin'—called Leoville—his last rendezvous in Phoenix Park, and the painful incident of her death at Sydney Parade Station.

CHARACTERS: Mr Duffy, who is described through his attitudes, his habits, his artistic and intellectual tendencies and his psychological idiosyncrasies—successively in Nietzschean,* Freudian† and medieval medical terms—rather than physically (as is usually the case with Joyce's characters in *Dubliners*), occupies most of the scene. Mrs Emily Sinico's husband and daughter are barely mentioned, but to the unfortunate lady herself half a page is devoted, besides what we learn in the newspaper paragraph relating her end. She is forty-three (slightly younger than Mr Duffy), has been married for twenty-two years to a sea-captain of distant Italian origin, has an oval face, striking eyes and a defiant gaze, and a taste for music.

STRUCTURE AND PLOT: The first section of the story is devoted to the presentation of Mr James Duffy, a confirmed bachelor, and his adventureless life. Adventure comes in part 2 with the chance meeting with Mrs Sinico. They see each other at concerts, make appointments, and he finally visits her regularly at her home. Their friendship grows, he shares his intellectual life with her, she enjoys the break in her solitude but one night she makes the mistake of catching up his hand passionately and pressing it to her cheek. He leaves her. Four years later, Mr Duffy reads in the paper of the lady's death. She has been knocked down by a train while in a state of intoxication. Mr Duffy's first reaction is one of disgust at such intemperance, and of self-righteousness. On second thoughts, however, he feels ill at ease and after a fit of self-pity realises the burden of loneliness.

SIGNIFICANCE: *(a)* A mock love-story'. As Donald T. Torchiana underlines: 'Chapelizod, South George's Street and the Magazine Hill, identified with the beginning, middle and end of the story, are also Dublin's three associations with Isolde, her Chapel, her tower and her

---

*Friedrich Wilhelm Nietzsche (1844–1900), a German philosopher who developed the idea of the superman and rejected traditional Christian values.
†Sigmund Freud (1856–1939), an Austrian psychiatrist who originated psychoanalysis, based on the free association of ideas and the analyses of dreams. He stressed the role of infantile sexuality in later development.

fount, all adding to the ironic application of the Tristan and Isolde story to Mr Duffy's mistake'.*

(b) A psychological study in the mechanism of paralysing self-absorption and refusal of passion. Mr Duffy is both more intelligent and more unpleasant than Maria (in 'Clay'): he has the support of Nietzsche to back his own attitudes or condemn those of his lady-friend, which does not prevent him from resorting also to clichés (like Maria, or Stanislaus Joyce of whom the author is making fun here), such as this one: 'Love between man and man is impossible because there must not be sexual intercourse, and friendship between man and woman is impossible because there must be sexual intercourse.'

It will be noticed how, in his environment and habits (particularly at the beginning of the story), he is presented as a monk, exactly as Maria has been as a nun, though here we have a more sinister type of religious person:

> He never gave alms to beggars ... He had neither companions nor friends, church nor creed. He lived his spiritual life without any communion with others, visiting his relatives at Christmas and escorting them to the cemetery when they died. He performed these two social duties for old dignity's sake.

Notice also 'He read it [the newspaper paragraph] not aloud, but moving his lip as a priest does when he reads the prayers Secreto.' Well can Mr Duffy conclude that he is 'outcast from life's feast'. Yet he goes through two epiphanies, one at the height of his relationship with Mrs Sinico: 'This union exalted him, wore away the rough edges of his character, emotionalised his mental life ... He thought that in her eyes he would ascend to an angelical stature', and the other when he is about to condemn himself and pity the other. But silence and darkness fall again.

NOTES AND GLOSSARY:

river: The Liffey, which plays such an important part in *Finnegans Wake* where Chapelizod also reappears, as the home of the Earwicker family

Maynooth Catechism: Maynooth, a few miles from Chapelizod, is the site of St Patrick's College, the chief seminary in Ireland and a constituent college of the National University. The Catechism, a treatise for instruction in the elements of the Catholic faith, in the form of question and answer, was ordered by the National Synod of Maynooth and approved for general use throughout the Irish Church

*In The Irish Short Story, ed. P. Rafroidi and T. Brown, Colin Smythe, Gerrards Cross, 1979, p.131.

Hauptmann:	Gerhart Hauptmann (1862–1946), German dramatist and novelist
Michael Kramer:	a play by Hauptmann, first published in 1900. Hauptmann presented a copy of it to Joyce in 1938. Both Duffy and Kramer are hermits incapable of communication
Bile Beans:	pills to alleviate a bilious condition
saturnine:	born under the influence of the planet Saturn: bilious and gloomy, melancholy (one of the four humours of medieval medicine)
Rotunda:	in Joyce's time, a theatre at the north end of O'Connell Street. It is now a cinema, the Ambassador
Earlsfort Terrace:	street at the southeast corner of St Stephen's Green where the Dublin International Exhibition Building (now part of the old buildings of University College) was located
Leghorn:	an Italian port (Livorno)
Parkgate:	the eastern gate to Phoenix Park, west of Dublin
the buff *Mail:*	buff, or yellow. The *Mail* was a Tory newspaper
Secreto:	*(Latin)* in secret. The 'Secret' is the prayer (which varies with the Masses) said silently over the offerings just before the 'Preface'
league:	a temperance organisation
Lucan:	a village farther on from Chapelizod on the Maynooth road
County Kildare:	the county next to County Dublin in the east of Ireland
the *Herald:*	*The Evening Herald,* a Dublin newspaper
Magazine Hill:	a hill near the Magazine Fort in Phoenix Park

Stories of public life

Ivy Day in the Committee Room

PUBLICATION: Eighth in the order of composition, this story was more or less completed by the end of August 1905, and first published with the rest of the collection—which it helped to delay because of the passage dealing with Edward VII (about which Joyce was to appeal to George V) and the original use of 'bloody' (later to be deleted) in the sentence which read: 'Here's this fellow come to the throne after his bloody owl mother keeping him out of it till the man was grey ...' The reference is to Queen Victoria, who reigned from 1837 to 1901.

SETTING: Date and place are suggested in the title. The day is 6 October, anniversary of the death of Charles Stewart Parnell (1846–91), which his admirers commemorate by wearing an ivy leaf. The year is 1902, as we are told of King Edward VII's intended visit within the next few months (he came in July 1903). The place is a Committee Room in Dublin, a room which serves as headquarters for agents who have been canvassing voters in favour of a certain Richard J. Tierney for the coming municipal by-election in the Royal Exchange Ward (where Aungier Street and Wicklow Street were located).

PLOT AND CHARACTERS: There is no plot proper but a desultory conversation (conveyed by means of dialogue) between eight persons on the subjects of politics (mostly), public gossip and parenthood, ending with the recital of a patriotic poem. The eight persons are: Old Jack, caretaker; Matthew O'Connor, canvasser; Joe Hynes, journalist; John Henchy, canvasser; Father Keon, free priest; the boy from Tierney's public house; Crofton, canvasser; Lyons, canvasser. Mr Henchy, the most active and unscrupulous of the Dubliners present, and Mr Hynes, the author of the poem on 'The Death of Parnell', are of particular interest (the former being more or less modelled on Joyce's own father), and the main character is a ghost: that of the great Irish leader whom W.B. Yeats, among others, was to celebrate in his turn, notably in his poem 'Come gather round me, Parnellites':

> Come gather round me, Parnellites,
> And praise our chosen man ...
>
> And here's a cogent reason,
> And I have many more,
> He fought the might of England
> And saved the Irish poor,
> Whatever good a farmer's got
> He brought it all to pass;
> And here's another reason,
> That Parnell loved a lass.   (*Collected Poems*, p.355)

SIGNIFICANCE:
(a) A study in the paralysis of Irish political life following Parnell's death, conveyed by contrast between times 'when there was some life' and the present situation when no-one is worth fighting for (see O'Connor symbolically burning Tierney's card to light a cigarette) and no ideal is left.
(b) An indictment of present-day Ireland living in the dark, without thought: 'Mr Crofton ... was silent for two reasons. The first reason, sufficient in itself, was that he had nothing to say ...'; real spirituality (Keon is perhaps not even a priest at all); social or political choice;

interested only in elementary desires: drink (note the derisive 'poks' which punctuate the conversation), money and petty scandals; desiring nothing higher than respectability; snobbish; apt to betrayal to the point of welcoming the King of England and forgiving him—see 'he's a bit of a rake'—worse behaviour than that which brought about Parnell's fall; the victim of slavery all around.

(c) This is perhaps Joyce's most unified story (unity of time and place, unity of theme) although the setting was provided for him by his brother.*

NOTES AND GLOSSARY:

P.L.G.:	Poor Law Guardian, an elected administrator in charge of local relief
Christian Brothers:	a teaching order already mentioned in 'Araby'. Joyce attended one of their schools for a while, although he did not like to remember it as he preferred the more intellectual and fashionable Jesuits
cocks him up:	(slang) gives him inflated ideas
a sup taken:	drunk too much
amn't, says ...:	note the language
Freemason:	the Masonic order has secret rites supposedly performed in the dark
tinker:	gypsy, beggar and robber
Corporation:	Municipal Council
shoneens:	(Irish) would-be gentlemen
handle to his name:	title
hunker-sliding:	laziness
German monarch:	the British Royal Family is of German origin
kowtowing:	or kotowing, to act in an obsequious manner, like the Chinese who touch the ground with the forehead as an expression of worship. (The word is of Chinese origin)
spondulics:	(slang) money
Musha, usha:	exclamation of surprise in Irish
nominators:	those who suggest the names for an election
hand-me-down shop:	or reach-me-down, a shop where second-hand clothes are sold
moya:	an ironic exclamation
stump up:	(slang) pay up
twig:	(slang) understand
decent skin:	good fellow

*Stanislaus Joyce: My Brother's Keeper, The Viking Press, New York, 1958, pp.205–6.

hillsiders and Fenians: the two words were used for the members of the Irish revolutionary organisation called after the warriors of the Fenian saga (or saga of Finn)

Castle: Dublin Castle, the seat of the English government in Ireland

Major Sirr: (1764–1841) sometime chief of the Dublin police; he helped to suppress the 1798 rebellion

the Black Eagle: a pub

Kavanagh's: a pub

knock it out: makes end meet

I thought he was the dozen of stout: I thought it was the boy who was bringing the bottles of beer

goster: *(slang)* noisy talk

Alderman: an elected member of the town Corporation

yerra: a mild oath

hop-o'-my thumb: used contemptuously of a small or young man

Mansion House: residence of the Lord Mayor of Dublin, elected annually by the Corporation

vermin: a malapropism (or deliberate pun?) on 'ermine' with which the ceremonial robe of a Lord Mayor is trimmed

Wisha: an exclamation of surprise in Irish

tally: amount

Any bottles?: empties from the previous delivery

tinpot way: a cheap ineffectual way

thin edge: 'The thin end of the wedge is to be feared' is the usual proverb

Talk of the devil: the proverb continues 'and he'll appear'

Did the cow calve?: is there something to celebrate?

toff: a swell

Parnell: see 'Setting' above. Parnell had been opposed to an official reception of Edward VII (then Prince of Wales) in 1885

the old one: Queen Victoria. Henchy (or Joyce) is wrong, though, for she had visited Ireland in 1900

play fair: note the irony of the reference to that alleged quality of the English in connection with Parnell, 'the Chief'

renege: desert, betray

green flag: green is the traditional colour of Ireland and was forbidden by the English

fawning priests: the Roman Catholic hierarchy proved to be the allies of the English Conservatives in the downfall of Parnell. See the 'Christmas scene' in *A Portrait of the Artist as a Young Man*

A Mother

PUBLICATION: 1914, with the rest of the collection. Finished by late September 1905.

SETTING: Mrs Kearney's house; the Antient Concert Rooms in Dublin.

CHARACTERS: Mrs Kearney, née Devlin, a middle-aged woman of bourgeois origin who has married a sober, thrifty, pious and docile bootmaker after the failure of her romantic dreams; her husband; her meek daughter, Kathleen, with an interest in Irish and music. Friends of theirs, like Miss Healy who will turn traitor. The secretary (Mr Fitzpatrick) and assistant secretary (Mr Holohan) of the *Eire Abu* Society (a patriotic and cultural organisation whose Gaelic motto meant 'Ireland to Victory'!). A number of *artistes*: Mr Duggan, the bass; Mr Bell, the second tenor; Madam Glynn, the soprano (who 'looked as if she had been resurrected from an old stage wardrobe')—part-time entertainers all, with little or no talent. Then there is Miss Beirne and Mr O'Madden Burke (who reappears in *Ulysses*), an ignorant journalist.

PLOT: Mr Holohan proposes that Mrs Kearney's daughter should be the accompanist at a series of four grand concerts which his society is organising. Kathleen is to receive eight guineas for it. Mrs Kearney, out of love for money and social climbing, enthusiastically accepts. In spite of her endeavours things do not turn out the way she had expected: on the first night the audience is poor, in quality and quantity, and the *artistes* are no good. It is then decided that there will only be three concerts with special efforts to secure a full house on the Saturday night, a decision which Mrs Kearney will accept only if it doesn't alter the original contract.

I Iowever, although she moves heaven and earth, she gets only four pounds (half the sum minus four shillings) before the first part of the last performance, and refuses to have Kathleen play in the rest of the evening if she is not paid the remainder of the money during the interval. As nothing comes, she threatens all and sundry and leaves the concert room with husband and daughter while the first chords of Miss Healy's accompaniment (she has 'kindly' accepted to replace her friend) are heard.

SIGNIFICANCE:
(a) Although the setting is Dublin, the capital city, this is a scene from *provincial* life where so-called 'cultural' activities are second-rate and bear witness to the paralysis of the arts.
(b) A post-mortem on Joyce's own dead singing career.
(c) A satire on Irish tastes at the turn of the century (the revival of the language, romanticism ...).

(d) A social satire on bourgeois values, the cult of money, pretension, social climbing, snobbery.
(e) A comedy of character with an indictment of the dominant female and the subdued male, and of girls' education and its inadequacy to real life.
(f) With 'Grace' (the last story of 'public life'), the most patently sneering of Joyce's tales of Dublin life.

NOTES AND GLOSSARY:

Holohan: on Holohan's and Kathleen's name, see the Introduction to these Notes

Eire Abu: see 'Characters' above

game leg: lame leg

every First Friday: to receive communion in honour of the Sacred Heart every first Friday of the month was, before the Council, a fairly recent Catholic practice quite strong in Ireland. Christ was supposed to have promised St Margaret Mary Alacoque (see 'Eveline') that anyone faithful to that devotion for nine consecutive first Fridays would not die without the sacraments

the Academy: the Royal Academy of Music

Skerries, Howth, Greystones: seaside holiday resorts near Dublin

the Irish Revival: included not only a literary Renaissance with writers such as Yeats (the author of *The Countess Cathleen* and *Kathleen ni Houlihan*—hence the reference to Mrs Kearney's determination 'to take advantage of her daughter's name') but, since the foundation of the *Gaelic League* in 1893, a renewed interest in Ireland's original language which few people, however, outside the Gaeltacht, were even able to speak properly (hence the fact that Kathleen and her friends merely say 'good-bye' to each other in Irish)

Pro-cathedral: the Dublin church used by Catholics as (= pro) a cathedral, the traditional ones (St Patrick's and Christ Church) belonging to the Protestant Church of Ireland

charmeuse: trimming

Brown Thomas's: a lace and linen shop

Maritana: a popular sentimental opera by the Irish composer William Vincent Wallace (1812–65), with libretto by Edward Fitzball. It was first performed in Dublin in 1846

Feis Ceoil:	an annual music festival begun in 1897 and still in existence. It is held each time at a different place. In 1904 Joyce competed
the *Freeman:*	the *Freeman's Journal*, a Dublin morning newspaper
Mansion House:	see 'Ivy Day'
Mrs Pat Campbell:	Mrs Patrick Campbell, née Béatrice Stella Tanner (1865–1940), one of the greatest British actresses of her day. She played an important part in George Bernard Shaw's life and plays
Killarney:	a sentimental song by the Irish composer Michael W. Balfe (1808–70)
ride roughshod:	tyrannise

Grace

PUBLICATION: 1914, with the rest of the collection. In the original arrangement it was to be the last story of the volume. Written mostly in 1905, although partly revised in 1906 after Joyce had done additional research in the Biblioteca Vittorio Emanuele in Rome for the theological parts of the story.

CHARACTERS: Mr Kernan, a dignified commercial traveller, originally from Protestant stock, and with a tendency to drink too much; his wife, an active, practical woman of middle age with no illusions and little fantasy; his respectable friends: Mr Power, employed by the Royal Irish Constabulary in Dublin Castle; Mr Cunningham, unfortunate in love but fairly well versed in philosophy; Mr M'Coy, now secretary to the City Coroner after tasting a variety of jobs; Mr Fogarty, a modest grocer; a policeman; a Jesuit, Father Purdon (modelled upon an English priest, Father Bernard Vaughan); a few other penitents among whom a certain Harford, a moneylender, stands out.

SETTING AND PLOT: Both Stuart Gilbert and Stanislaus Joyce have emphasised the fact that 'Grace' was planned with the pattern of Dante's *Divine Comedy* in mind.

In part 1, Mr Kernan falls down the steps of the lavatory in a Dublin bar. This is the descent into hell from which, while he is on the point of being arrested for drunkenness, he is rescued by Mr Power who takes him back to his wife and children in Glasnevin Road.

In part 2, Mr Kernan is seen in the Purgatory of the sickroom where his friends come to plot his salvation by means of a retreat which they will all attend 'to wash the pot', a decision not easily reached by the ex-Protestant and drunkard, and which therefore takes some building up of the atmosphere by way of a long discussion on Church history and theology—in which Joyce mockingly piles up half-truths and mistakes fairly difficult for the layman to sort out. A study such as Robert M. Adams: *Surface and Symbol*, Oxford University Press, New York, 1962, pp.177–81, gives a clearer, detailed view of the subject.

In part 3, where the scene is the Jesuit Church in Gardiner Street attended by a large congregation of gentlemen all well-dressed and orderly, listening to Father Purdon developing the text of the Scriptures 'The children of this world are wiser in their generation than the children of the light', we reach Paradise at last, even though with a slight doubt as to the everlasting quality of the 'grace' dispensed therein.

SIGNIFICANCE:

(a) This is the last story of public life, with religious paralysis as its subject, religion appearing in Dublin as debased by its utilitarian aspect and its closeness to superstition; see this definition of Mrs Kernan's faith: 'She believed steadily in the Sacred Heart as the most generally *useful* of all Catholic devotions and approved of the sacraments. Her faith was bounded by her kitchen, but, if she was put to it, she could believe also in the banshee and in the Holy Ghost.' Notice its ignorance and lack of sound theological backing (see the friends' discussion), its secular reduction to accounts of bad or good deeds (see Father Purdon's sermon).

(b) The story is one of Joyce's most successful sets of parodies (*The Divine Comedy*, learned dialogues, sermons, mock-heroic presentation of the lavatory episode, etc).

(c) It is the best example, in *Dubliners*, of the author's ambiguous attitude to his masters, the Jesuits, whom he at once revered and longed to ridicule.

(d) It is a story in which the point of view throughout is Joyce's and he intervenes continuously with ironic comments on persons and situations.

(e) It is a story which announces *Ulysses*, and is akin to it through mood and characters, and yet links up with the very first title in *Dubliners* through the theme of simony.

NOTES AND GLOSSARY:

to indite: to put into written words

an outsider: an outside car, a jaunting car, on which passengers sit back-to-back on benches facing at right angles to the driver's seat

a silk hat of some decency: probably an allusion to the song 'That Hat Me Father Wore' where the following line was to be found: It's a relic of old dacency, is the hat me father wore

to pass muster: to come up to the required standard

Blackwhite:	probably some merchant or salesman unknown to all except the locals
E.C.:	East Central, one of London's old mailing districts
Constabulary:	police
Star of the Sea:	one of the names of the Virgin Mary in the litanies devoted to her praise (*Latin*, Stella Maris)
Sandymount:	a seaside suburb near Dublin
pale:	in Anglo-Irish, the word was used to describe the district round Dublin where English domination was supreme. To connect it with Mr Kernan's less than perfect allegiance to the Catholic Church is, of course, one of Joyce's pointed ironies in this story
the banshee:	an old fairy-woman whose wailing foretells the death of someone. Part of the Irish folk tradition
Bona-fide:	(*Latin*) in good faith. Publicans are allowed to serve drinks on Sundays to actual, legitimate travellers but not to local customers
peloothered:	drunk. Possibly a misreading by the printer of the anglicised Gaelic word 'phloothered' which has the same meaning
squared:	conciliated
strait-laced:	excessively rigid, scrupulous or prudish
bostooms:	a bostoon (or bosthoon)—from the Irish *bastún*, a switch of green rushes—it means 'a country lout'
omadhauns:	fools (also from the Irish)
yahoos:	ape-like human beings in Book IV of Jonathan Swift's (1667–1745) *Gulliver's Travels* (1726) where the only noble creatures are horses (Houyhnhnms). According to one interpretation the Yahoos represented the Irish, according to another the English invaders
hubby:	husband
M'Auley's:	a pub
retreat:	a period of withdrawal from the world for prayer and meditation
to wash the pot:	to wipe the slate clean
reel:	a dance
The General of the Jesuits:	the Society of Jesus was organised by his founder, Saint Ignatius Loyola, a soldier, along military lines. Hence the fact that its superior is called 'General'. He does not 'stand next to the Pope' being no part of the normal hierarchy of cardinals, etc, but it is true that he is an influential person responsible only to the Supreme Pontiff

reformed:	'Every other order of the Church had to be reformed at some time or other, but the Jesuit Order was never once reformed.' True, and meaningless, such orders as were reformed (monks' and friars') being much older than the Jesuits', founded only in 1540
secular priests:	the Catholic clergy is composed of secular priests, living in the 'world' (*saeculum* in Latin), in charge of parishes and the like, not subject to a specific rule and taking no 'vows' (only 'promises'); and of 'religious' or 'regular' priests belonging to an order and living together in a house or monastery. The training of members of the regular clergy is longer (especially the Jesuits') and they are supposed to have a much better intellectual level, although they rarely reach the highest honours (bishop, cardinal, Pope) generally reserved for secular priests. The opposition between the two bodies is well-known
Father Purdon:	Purdon Street was notorious for its brothels
Father Tom Burke:	an Irish Dominican friar (1830–82). Another famous quarrel in the Catholic Church, mostly about questions of theological interpretations of the problem of grace and liberty, is that between the Jesuits and the sons of St Dominic. Hence the Jesuit-inspired remark 'he wasn't much of a theologian'
pit:	this word, used only in connection with the theatre and never with a church (which has a 'nave'), is purposely put in Mr Kernan's mouth to make fun of his ignorance in religious matters. (He is only a 'convert')
The Prisoner of the Vatican:	Pope Pius IX (who reigned from 1846 to 1878), Pope Leo XIII (1878–1903) and their immediate successors considered themselves as prisoners in protest against the seizure of their temporal powers in 1870
an Orangeman:	used here with the meaning 'a Protestant' although, technically, an Orangeman is a member of the Orange Society founded in 1795 and belongs to a particularly intolerant brand of Protestantism
the Mother of God:	Protestants believe in the mother of God but don't make her the object of a special worship
motto:	*Lux upon Lux* with its mixture of Latin and English is evidently impossible. *Lumen in Coelo* (Light in the sky) was attributed to Leo XIII while Pius IX had been given *Crux de cruce* (Cross from a cross)

Latin poetry: Leo XIII, no great scholar, did in fact write a (bad) Latin poem on the invention of the photograph

penny-a-week school: a National school. See 'Encounter'

turf ... oxter: peat (a natural fuel, a country symbol) under his arm

Great minds ... Madness: a commonplace remark versified by John Dryden (1631–1700) in *Absalom and Achitophel* (1681–2), I–163, in slightly different terms:

Great wits are sure to madness near allied,
And thin partitions do their bounds divide

knocker: standard

ex cathedra ... **infallible:** since the Vatican Council's proclamation of 1870, under Pius IX, the Pope is supposed to be infallible when he speaks from his chair ('cathedra') of office on matters of faith. Many members of the Church privately opposed that particular dogma which has caused havoc ever since, but in 1870 only two dissenters voted against: *not* John MacHale (1791–1881), the Irish Archbishop of Tuam, who was conveniently absent (in spite of what Mr Cunningham has to say on the subject) but Bishop Riccio, an Italian, and Fitzgerald, an American. As for 'Dolling' or 'Dowling'—in fact Johann Döllinger (1799–1890)—although he did oppose the doctrine of papal infallibility, he was neither a cardinal nor a member of the Vatican Council of 1869–70

sacred college: the college of cardinals

conclave: the assembly of cardinals met for the election of the pope (or the place where they meet). Neither term has any relevance to a Council

Sir John Gray: a protestant patriot (1816–75) owner of *The Freeman's Journal.* His statue stands on O'Connell Street in Dublin. Edmund Dwyer Gray was his son

taped: classified

candles: much in use in Catholic liturgy but an ex-Protestant must draw the line there

baptismal vows: the promises made by the godparents at the time of a child's baptism must be renewed now and again by the conscientious adult

lay-brother: religious orders have members who do not become priests and are in charge of menial chores

speck of red light: the sanctuary light which indicates the presence of the Blessed Sacrament (the consecrated Host)

quincunx:	a set of five things (or persons) so placed that four occupy the corners and the fifth the centre of a square or rectangle
surplice:	a short choir vestment of white linen, generally with wide sleeves, worn by priests over the black cassock
pulpit:	a raised structure in a church from which sermons are delivered

For the children of this world ...: the text is taken from the Gospel of St Luke, 16:8–9, and is a particularly appropriate one for businessmen; for a Jesuit (they were often accused of worldliness and compromise with the world of money); and for the author's desire to disclose the debasement of religious life

Death (and resurrection?)

The Dead

PUBLICATION: First published with the rest of the collection but no part of the original plan, this longest story (or 'novella') in *Dubliners* was written in Trieste in 1907.

SETTING: The Misses Morkans' house where Miss Kate, Miss Julia and their niece Mary Jane give their Christmas party; a room in the Gresham Hotel where Gabriel Conroy and his wife Gretta are to spend the night.

CHARACTERS: As 'The Dead', in its first two parts, describes a party, quite a number of people are presented or mentioned. There are the hostesses, already referred to; Gabriel: 'a stout, tallish young man with glossy black hair and glasses'; Gretta, a rather beautiful young woman — although Gabriel's mother once spoke of her as merely 'country-cute'; Lily, the housemaid. Then the guests, particularly Miss Ivors, a university teacher like Gabriel, fanatically in love with her own country; Freddy Malins, a drunkard; Mr Bartell D'Arcy, a singer; Mr Browne, an English Protestant addicted to bad quips.

STRUCTURE AND PLOT: 'The Dead' has the usual division into three parts, indicated by Joyce himself; arrival of the guests and first dances; Gabriel's own dance with Miss Ivors, supper and speech; last song, departure, hotel scene with the revelation of Gretta's past love.

As usual, this story has also been described as another *Divine Comedy*, the Morkan household being Gabriel's hell, the carriage trip to the Gresham serving as a period of purgation, the hotel scene of revelation forming an ironic paradise. Such a theory does not correspond with the actual divisions, however.

'The Dead' is, in fact, the working out, in three stages, of a unified theme, that of a man's realisation of his psychological paralysis—or egotism—which is broken down by three failures or rebukes, one in each part of the story: (1) Lily's refusal of a tip: Gabriel's failure as a gentleman, (2) Miss Ivor's use of the abusive term 'West Briton': Gabriel's failure as an Irishman, (3) Gretta's withdrawal into the past and her revelation: Gabriel's failure as a man, a lover and a husband. He is then left alone (his wife is fast asleep although what he had wanted was to awaken her sexually) to meditate on the living and the dead, in a conclusion that is ambiguous enough for some readers to think that he yields to the final paralysis symbolised by the snow, and others—like the present writer—to believe he rises from the shades through generosity, love and a closer union with nature.

SIGNIFICANCE AND POINTS OF INTEREST:
(a) See previous paragraph for general meaning.
(b) See introduction for the significance of the West of Ireland and autobiographical elements.*
(c) See Part 3 (Texture) for portrait technique, lexical accuracy, stylistic mimetism. The cosmic imagery of 'The Dead' is also interesting to study as is (still from the point of view of style) the superb pastiche of 'after dinner' speeches. All the clichés are there, from the humility of the beginning ('a task for which my poor powers as a speaker are all too inadequate') to the triteness of the final toast, not forgetting the couplet on Irish hospitality, the opposition between generations, the mythological allusions or such hackneyed images as 'our path through life is strewn with many sad memories'. The passage is a significant one, to be compared, in its insincerity, to the sincerity of the last two pages. Proper names may also be of interest (see note on Michael Furey, p.66).
(d) Among literary reminiscences that Joyce may have incorporated, George Moore's *Vain Fortune* (1891) has been mentioned for the end, except for the snow image probably borrowed from the 12th Book of *The Iliad*. D. T. Torchiana recalls that 'John Kelleher's justly famous essay "Irish History and Mythology in J. Joyce's 'The Dead'" cleverly establishes the mythic centre of the final story as the fate of King Conaire in the saga "The Destruction of Da Derga's Hostel",' and sees in Gabriel a resurrection of the Patron Saint of Ireland, Saint Patrick.
(e) Finally the essential role of Gabriel (and Gretta) should not blind the reader to the other values of the story, which is also a piece of social criticism, a picture of musical life in Dublin at the turn of the century, a portrait of other characters, some deceased, some moribund, some living-dead, and a reshuffling of many of the themes already used in the

*Also: P. Rafroidi: 'James et Nora, Gabriel et Gretta; Richard et Bertha: Autobiographie et Fiction dans "The Dead" et *Exiles* de Joyce', *Etudes Irlandaises*, V, Lille, 1980.

previous stories, including the themes of money, financial decline, class destinctions, and so on.

NOTES AND GLOSSARY:

Stoney Batter: a northern suburb of Dublin

Usher's Island: a quay on the Liffey

Kingstown, Dalkey: fashionable seaside resorts on the coast south of Dublin. Kingstown is now Dun Laoghaire

Adam and Eve's: a Dublin church

under the influence: of drink; intoxicated

Browning ... above the heads: the poetry of Robert Browning (1812–89) has a reputation for difficulty

the Melodies: Thomas Moore's *Irish Melodies* (1807–34), a much more accessible kind of verse.

Monkstown, Merrion: Monkstown is about nine miles south-east of Dublin; Merrion is half-way between

dumb-bells: weight bars used for physical exercise

gutta-percha: *(Malay):* 'tree of the gum', that is, rubber; what galoshes are made of

Christy Minstrels: Edwin T. Christy was famous for his minstrel shows

the Gresham: a fashionable Dublin hotel

screwed: drunk

wizen: wizened, shrivelled, withered

thither: 'there'. Note the deliberate archaism of the vocabulary

quadrille: a square dance of French origin

the balcony scene: in Shakespeare's play *Romeo and Juliet* it is the second scene of Act 2

the tower: the Tower of London where the young sons of Edward IV are supposed to have been murdered. After *Romeo and Juliet*, the allusion here is to an historical play of Shakespeare's: *Richard III*

tabinet: an Irish watered fabric of silk and wool resembling poplin

mulberry: a dark purple colour like that of the fruit of the same name

Balbriggan: about twenty miles north of Dublin. Gabriel and his clerical brother live in opposite directions

The Royal University: established in 1882, the ancestor of the National University

lancer: a variety of quadrille

The Daily Express: a Conservative paper opposed to the nationalist cause, hence Miss Ivor's rebuke to Gabriel who has been writing in it under the initials G.C.

West Briton: not a real Irishman, but an Englishman living in Ireland, or an Anglicised Irishman

Bachelor's Walk ... Aston's Quay: two quays on opposite sides of the Liffey just before O'Connell Bridge; the bookshops mentioned were actual ones

Aran Isles: three famous islands off the West Coast. Gaelic and a primitive way of life still prevailed in them and promotors of the Irish revival, such as J. M. Synge, went there on pilgrimage

Kathleen Kearny: see 'A Mother'

Connacht: or Connaught, the western province of Ireland from which not only Gretta Conroy but Nora Joyce came

Galway: the capital city of Connaught

the Park: Phoenix Park

the Wellington Monument: in Phoenix Park. Arthur Wellesley, Duke of Wellington (1769–1852) was born in Ireland, but refused to consider himself as Irish. 'The fact of being born in a stable does not make a man a horse', he used to say. That Gabriel should be thinking of him after the incident with Miss Ivors is certainly no coincidence

Three Graces, Paris: the allusion is to Greek mythology where Paris had to choose to which of three goddesses (Hera, Athena, Aphrodite) he would award the gold apple, maliciously thrown by Eris (Discord). He chose the goddess of Love, Aphrodite

Arrayed for the Bridal: a song in Bellini's opera *I Puritani*, 1835

women out of the choirs: in his famous *Motu Proprio* of 1903, Pope Pius X (canonised since then) tried to restore some order in the liturgy and forbade, among other things, the use of instruments other than the organ in church, and the presence of women in choirs

whipper-snappers: insignificant young fellows

the other persuasion: Protestantism

Beannacht libh: a farewell salutation in Irish

The Theatre Royal: in Hawkins Street, Dublin

The Gaiety: also a Dublin Theatre, on South King Street

legitimate: 'grand' opera, as opposed to Variety

Mignon: an opera by the French composer Ambroise Thomas (1811–96), first produced in Paris in 1866

Tietjens ... etc: opera singers of note, though none was to become so famous as the celebrated tenor Enrico Caruso (1874–1921)

the Old Royal: a Dublin theatre destroyed by fire in 1880

Let me Like a Soldier Fall: from the opera *Maritana* (1846) by William Vincent Wallace (already mentioned in 'A Mother')

Dinorah: also called *Le Pardon de Ploermel* (1859), an opera by Giacomo Meyerbeer (1791–1864)

Lucrezia Borgia: an opera (1833) by Gaetano Donizetti (1797–1848)

Parkinson: probably an invented name

Mount Melleray: a reformed Cistercian ('Trappist') abbey in the South of Ireland. In Ireland, Cistercian monks give priority among their guests to those who want to stop drinking

coffins: as they follow the rule of St Benedict in a rather literal way, Cistercian monks sleep in their habits — but not in their coffins! The idea has perhaps been suggested by the fact that when they are buried, there is no lid to the coffin

Fifteen Acres: also part of Phoenix Park

camaraderie: *(French)* companionship

Back Lane: a street not very far from Usher's Island

King Billy: William III (of Orange), the winner of the Battle of the Boyne (1690)

Trinity College: the place is so central and so well known that Browne's question to the cabman is ludicrous

Terra-cotta: brownish-red, the colour of earthenware pottery

O, the rain …: from the Irish song 'The Lass of Aughrim'

The Four Courts: the Irish law courts across the Liffey from Merchant's Quay

Winetavern Street: in the same district

Dan: the affectionate (or ironical, as here) diminutive given to Daniel O'Connell (1775–1847), the 'liberator' who won Catholic Emancipation for Ireland in 1829

Henry Street: a crowded shopping street by the G.P.O.

Michael Furey: Nora's suitor, who had known a similar fate to that of Furey, was called Michael Bodkin (a Galway name). Is it because of Michael that Joyce has called his hero Gabriel (both archangels)?*

Oughterard: a village some twenty miles north of Galway

Nuns' Island: off the western coast. Nora Barnacle (Mrs Joyce) had lived there

Bog of Allen: a large peat lowland south-west of Dublin

Shannon: crossing this river brings one to the West of Ireland

---

*Florence L. Walzl: 'Gabriel and Michael: The Conclusion of "The Dead"' (*Dubliners*, ed. Scholes & Litz, The Viking Press, New York, 1969, pp.423–4).

Part 3

Commentary

The semantics of *Dubliners*

Subject

Joyce had in mind to compose an overall presentation of Ireland, in which *Dubliners* was to be followed by *Provincials*, the latter probably an ironical title for an admirer of the Jesuits since it had already been used, in the seventeenth century, by their arch enemy Blaise Pascal. Joyce would certainly have been at a loss in presenting the Irish provinces, of which he knew nothing at first hand, and his ignorance may account for the fact that the second project never materialised. But the first did, and its subject is apparently quite clear, both from its title and from what we read about it in Joyce's own correspondence. 'I do not think that any writer has yet presented Dublin to the world', he wrote from Trieste to Grant Richards on 15 October 1905, and added, 'It has been a capital of Europe for thousands of years, it is supposed to be the second city of the British Empire' [Ireland had not yet gained its freedom from England] and it is nearly three times as big as Venice. Moreover, on account of many circumstances which I cannot detail here, the expression "Dubliner" seems to me to have some meaning, and I doubt whether the same can be said for such words as "Londoner" and "Parisian", both of which have been used by writers as titles.'

Dublin, then, is the subject of the collection, or more precisely, the inhabitants of the capital of Ireland, viewed, according to Joyce's own pronouncements, in their childhood (first three stories), adolescence (stories 4 to 7), mature life (stories 8 to 11), public life (stories 12, 13, 14) and death (last story).

Purpose

The question arises whether the novelty of the subject (and it was not as new as all that: Dublin and Dubliners had not been absent from nineteenth-century Irish fiction) can be considered sufficient reason for Joyce to have embarked on it. Was his purpose mere naturalistic presentation? Or was the Dublin setting and the analysis of the lives of Dubliners an ideal means of self-expression—witness the autobiographical elements we have pointed out in the Introduction, and others we may have left out: the hoped-for and dreaded vocation to the priesthood ('The Sisters'), the experience of first love ('Araby') and degradation ('An Encounter'), the projection into the future of the person he would have become if he had stayed in Dublin as a clerk in an office, a singer, or even a fairly successful reviewer ('The Dead')? Or was it revelation: the bringing forth of the (first) Gospel according to St James? Again judging from Joyce's letters, there is no doubt that the last hypothesis is the right one. This he stated negatively when he remarked of Maupassant in a letter to Stanislaus dated 19 July 1905: 'Maupassant writes very well, of course, but I am afraid that his moral sense is rather obtuse, and, in a positive way, in a number of passages such as this letter of 1904 to Constantine P. Curran, 'I am writing a series of epicleti.' Joyce, for all his knowledge of religion, may be wrong in the use of this particular word, which should be 'epicleses' if taken from Latin, or 'epicleseis' if modelled on the Greek, but the idea remains of providing invocations, as they are to be found in the Eastern Rite of the Church, in which the Holy Ghost is besought to transform the bread and the wine into the body and blood of Christ—to transcend, in other words, the appearances of the material world in order to reach the spiritual. Joyce put it another way when replying to Grant Richards, who had suggested that he should delete certain words or episodes: 'If I eliminate them what becomes of the *Chapter of the moral history of my country*?' 'I fight to retain them because I believe that in composing my chapter of moral history in exactly the way I have composed it I have taken *the first step towards the spiritual liberation of my country*' [present author's italics] (May 20, 1906).

Some critics have even gone farther than this generalisation, suggesting, like Brewster Ghiselin in 'The Unity of *Dubliners*', that:

> In the first three stories, in which the protagonists are presumably innocent, the theological virtues faith, hope, and love, in the conventional order, are successively displayed in abeyance and finally in defeat.
>
> In the fourth story, the main character, Eveline, lacking the strength of faith, hope, and love, wavers in an effort to find a new life and, failing in the cardinal virtue of fortitude, remains in Dublin, short of her goal and weakened in her spiritual powers and defenses against evil.
>
> In the fifth through the eleventh stories the seven deadly sins, pride, covetousness, lust, envy, anger, gluttony, and sloth are portrayed successively in action usually with other sins adjacent on the list.*

Pride is the subject of 'After the Race'; covetousness or avarice that of

*In P. K. Garrett (ed.): *Twentieth Century Interpretations of 'Dubliners'*, Prentice Hall, Englewood Cliffs, N.J., 1968, p.62.

'Two Gallants'; lust or lechery that of 'The Boarding House'; envy is to be found in 'A Little Cloud'; anger in 'Counterparts'; greed, if not exactly gluttony, in 'Clay'; sloth in 'A Painful Case'. Professor Ghiselin goes on 'In the twelfth through the fourteenth stories, the subversion of the cardinal virtues . . . is displayed'. Perhaps, though, the concordance which Matthew Hodgart* establishes on similar lines as his predecessor, is a more convincing one: courage in 'Ivy Day', justice in 'A Mother', temperance in 'Grace', both critics accepting wisdom or magnanimity as characteristic of 'The Dead'.

Whichever is right (if either) or whether we should cling to Joyce's opinions alone, the moral purpose seems to be there all right, the only question being of Joyce's qualifications to act the moralist. Nor is there any incompatibility between self-expression and the description of others, or between so-called 'realistic' (or 'naturalistic') presentation of the world and the spiritual goal to be reached in reaction to what actually is. Quite the contrary, the reflection in the mirror of reality may be an incentive to seek the radiance of eternity—this, at any rate, is what Joyce implied in another letter to Richards, dated 23 June 1906: 'It is not my fault that the odour of ashpits and old weeds and offal hangs round my stories. I seriously believe that you will retard the course of civilisation in Ireland by preventing the Irish people from having one good look at themselves in my nicely polished looking-glass.' And he had insisted several times, probably in the same light, on 'the significance of trivial things.'

Theme

Whether Joyce wrote for the mere pleasure of writing, out of a deep need of self-expression, out of a spirit of revenge, or in order to improve mankind, there is no denying the presence in *Dubliners* of a major moral theme, that of *paralysis*, consciously introduced and obviously developed and denounced throughout the stories, in all its manifestations.

Joyce was barely twenty-one when he remarked to Stanislaus, 'What's the matter with you is that you're afraid to live. You and people like you. The city is suffering from hemiplegia of the will'† and in the letter on 'epicleti' already referred to, he added, 'I call the series *Dubliners* to betray the soul of that hemiplegia or paralysis which many consider a city.' A detailed analysis of the fifteen stories will further show that Joyce did not depart from his original project, as many authors often do.

The theme is introduced in the first sentence of the first piece—

*In his *James Joyce: A Student's Guide*, Routledge & Kegan Paul, London, 1978, p.45.
†Quoted by Stanislaus Joyce: *My Brother's Keeper*, The Viking Press, New York, 1958, p.248

'There was no hope for him this time: it was the third stroke', with the actual paralysis of the old priest and the fascination which the threatening word carries to the boy, not very different in this respect from Joyce himself—'it sounded to me like the name of some maleficent and sinful being. It filled me with fear, and yet I longed to be nearer to it and to look upon its deadly work'. And, according to one kind of interpretation at least, it can be considered as present in the last sentence of the very last story—'His [Gabriel's] soul swooned slowly as he heard the snow falling faintly through the universe and faintly falling, like the descent of their last end, upon all the living and the dead.'

Meanwhile the successive tales have presented a series of other occurrences of the theme: paralysis of action: see the motionless figure of Eveline, 'passive, like a helpless animal'; professional paralysis; political paralysis ('Ivy Day'); sexual ('An Encounter'); moral, intellectual and even verbal paralysis as shown in the recurrence of clichés—romantic ('Araby'), religious ('Grace') and literary (Gabriel's in 'The Dead').

Variations

All the variations of the theme seem nothing else than a study of the causes and consequences of paralysis, and—possibly—a study in remedies. Two causes are stressed over and over again: corruption and the search for false values. Corruption is essentially presented through money. Cash plays an astonishing role in many of the stories of *Dubliners*, as it did indeed in Joyce's own life where it created yet another dichotomy: a believer in spiritual values, Joyce was against all forms of materialism, but he hardly ever had enough for a living—not to mention his luxurious tastes in eating out and drinking, and his lordly attitudes whenever he could play the host. He therefore spent his life counting his pennies, borrowing from a number of people, particularly his brother, depending on the generosity of patrons, despising money and rich people and yet ever on the look-out to refill his purse.

'Counterparts' is interesting to study from this point of view as is 'After the Race'. But several other pieces have money as a central motif: 'Araby' (the boy cannot go to the bazaar as his uncle has not given him the expected florin which stands between him and the world of romance); 'Two Gallants', 'Clay', and 'A Mother'. Even 'The Dead' does not escape, with Gabriel awkwardly thrusting a coin into Lily's hands at the beginning of the story, while at the end, to cover his sexual embarrassment to Gretta in the hotel room, he mentions the fact that Malins has given him back a sovereign he lent him at Christmas. As for 'Grace' it offers the supreme form of corruption through money (already hinted at in the first story, 'The Sisters', with the word 'simony'), the corruption of the spiritual world itself, the Church debased by Father

Purdon so as to appear as a mere accountant's office. 'Well, I have verified my accounts. I find all well' ... 'Well, I have looked into my accounts. I find this wrong and this wrong. But, with God's grace, I will rectify this and this. I will set right my accounts.' Such grace that delivers people to the mammon of iniquity is but a means of establishing the paralysis of the soul which thrives on false values.

There are several other of these: false hopes, false ambitions: social ambition in particular (enough stress has not been laid on *Dubliners* as a kind of Irish *Book of Snobs* or the epic of a shabby-genteel society); yet further causes of a paralysis that results in arrest, sometimes imposed by external circumstances but oftener from within, through deficiency of impulse and power, and ends in total frustration. 'In every one of these fifteen case histories,' Harry Levin has remarked, 'we seem to be reading in the annals of frustration. Things almost happen. The characters are arrested in mid-air.'* M. Magalaner and R.M. Kain have written that 'to mention Joyce's main characters is to establish a gallery of thwarted escapees: Farrington, Eveline, Gabriel, Little Chandler, the boy in "An Encounter", and Polly Mooney's husband.'†

Conclusion

The looking-glass is unmistakable, but is it enough to initiate the 'spiritual liberation' which Joyce announced? He probably thought so. Translating St Thomas Aquinas's Latin *Pulchra sunt quae visa placent* (those things are beautiful the apprehension of which pleases), he contended, at the period of composition of *Dubliners*, in November 1904, that even the ugly can be beautiful if properly apprehended, and that 'apprehension' was the essential thing. The nature of the material is, in other words, of no importance to the *'epiphany'*, as he put it in *Stephen Hero*, the 'sudden spiritual manifestation, whether in the vulgarity of speech or of gesture or in a memorable phase of the mind itself, the perception, in a thing, or being of "its soul, its whatness" which even in the "commonest object" will then seem "radiant".' Only the perfect artist, however, can reach as far, not the paralysed victim of alien forces or inner compulsions. So the remedy to hemiplegia should in fact, be sought not in *Dubliners* but outside it, in *A Portrait of the Artist as a Young Man* where salvation lies in such aesthetic perceptions and in the creative escape ... of Stephen alone.

How is it, however, that we never, in *Dubliners*, experience the feeling of utter despair distilled by so much naturalistic writing? Is it not, in part, that Joyce's attitude of derision towards his paralytic capital is served by

James Joyce: A Critical Introduction, New Directions, Norfolk, Connecticut, 1960, pp.29–30.
†*Joyce: The Man, The Work, The Reputation*, Collier Books, New York, 1956, p.61.

too powerful a sense of the comic ever to coincide with the impotent acceptance of his characters? Is it not that even while describing the dead, that indomitable Irishman could never forget the everliving spirit that was to animate *Finnegans Wake*, and unconsciously awaited the resurrection he had taken so much trouble to deny? Perhaps, as we have already hinted and shall observe again, Joyce's last story does not point to a burial but is the intimation of an awakening.

Structure in *Dubliners*

Among Joyce's main characteristics are the taste and capacity for structure which he owed, or so he said, to his Jesuit masters from whom he 'learnt to arrange things in such a way' that they became 'easy to survey and to judge'.* These figure pre-eminently in *Dubliners* on both the level of the collection as a whole and on that of each individual story.

Overall structure

A collection of short stories may present a string of narratives with no other connection than the particular stamp of the author, or it may interweave the tales so as to build them into something that tends towards a novel in episodes, like Sherwood Anderson's (1876–1941) *Winesburg, Ohio* (1919) to which *Dubliners* has been compared. That a general plan presided over the conception of Joyce's series has already been emphasised in these pages. A few points may, however, be added. To begin with, Joyce seems never to have changed his mind on the order of the stories. Such an order derives from the moral structure defined in the previous chapter: a study of the spiritual paralysis of Dublin, first seen from a child's point of view, and afterwards experienced by adolescents becoming trapped, or adults realising they are already so. This is also the case of the whole community, as is shown in the stories of public life; 'The Dead' summarising the process and offering a conclusion ambiguous enough for readers not to be sure whether Joyce wants us to understand that the disease has become as widely spread as the snow, or that Gabriel, at least, has found a way out of the hemiplegia of his egotism by becoming a part of the general flux of nature.

Critical interpretations that do not have Joyce's authority to back them also point to a carefully-determined overall structure, whether it be 'moral' (for example, the virtues and sins mentioned in the previous chapter), or 'epic', 'pre-Ulyssean'—Richard Levin's and Charles Shattuck's viewpoint in 'First Flight to Ithaca',†—or based, as is

*Interview with August Suter, 1956. Quoted by Frank Budgen: 'Further Recollections of James Joyce', *Partisan Review*, XXIII, Fall, 1956, p.533.
†*Accent*, IV, 1944, pp.75–99; reprinted in S. Givens (ed.): *James Joyce: Two Decades of Criticism*, Vanguard Press, New York, 1948, pp.47–94.

suggested by Brewster Ghiselin, on a symbolic geography:

> It should be no surprise to discover in a book developing the theme of moral paralysis a fundamental structure of movements and stases ...
> It may be characterised briefly as an eastward trend, at first vague, quickly becoming dominant, then wavering, weakening and at last reversed. Traced in rough outline, the pattern is as follows: in a sequence of six stories, an impulse and movement eastward to the outskirts of the city or beyond; in a single story, an impulse to fly away upward out of a confining situation near the centre of Dublin; in a sequence of four stories, a gradual replacement of the impulse eastward by an impulse and movement westward; in three stories, a limited activity confined almost wholly within the central area of Dublin; and in the concluding story a movement eastward to the heart of the city, then, in vision only, far westward into death.
> Interpreted realistically, without recourse to symbol, this pattern may show at most the frustration of Dubliners unable to escape eastward, out of the seaport and overseas, to a more living world ...
> Understood in its symbolic import, however, the eastward motion or the desire for it takes on a much more complicated and precise significance.*

This is a significance which the critic seeks and finds in the life-force of the East, admitted both by the pagans who worshipped the rising sun and the Christians who have always turned their churches and their hearts towards that location of Eden.

The obvious mistake, however, of the 'epic' view is to see *Dubliners* as if Joyce had already created and revealed the world of *Ulysses*, the type of mistake that critics, mostly American, make when viewing Blake's *Songs of Innocence* not only in the light of his next experiences but in those of *Jerusalem* and *The Four Zoas*. The mistake of the symbolical interpretation is to place itself completely out of the Irish context, where the West obviously has the reverse significance and value from the one current in Texas. But, whether erroneous or true, such theories do confirm that *Dubliners* is perceived by all as a whole, which is all that matters here. Similarities of patterns, echoes and links between the various stories afford extra material evidence of such a unity. J.W. Corrington† and Hugh Kenner‡ have both brought together the first and the last pieces of the collection—so as to underline 'the almost circular motion of the stories in narrative as well as in theme'. J.W. Corrington, who has used the expression, adds:

*'The Unity of *Dubliners*', in P.K. Garrett (ed.): *Twentieth Century Interpretations of 'Dubliners'*, Prentice Hall, Englewood Cliffs, N.J., 1968, p.68.
†In Clive Hart (ed.): *James Joyce's 'Dubliners'*, Faber & Faber, London, 1969, p.17.
‡*Dublin's Joyce*, University of Indiana Press, Bloomington, Indiana, 1966, p.63.

'The Sisters' starts in darkness with a boy staring at a window, speaking of the dead, seeing the window lighted 'faintly', feeling his 'soul receding into some pleasant and vicious region'. Similarly, at the end of ... 'The Dead', Gabriel Conroy stares at the window where snow falls 'faintly' in the darkness, thinking of the dead, 'his soul had approached that region where dwell the vast hosts of the dead'.

Both stories are, in Hugh Kenner's phrase, 'dominated by two wraith-like sisters'. In the first story, a priest lies dead in his coffin; in 'The Dead', guests at the Misses Morkans' party speak of an order of monks who sleep in their coffins.

More evident still are the meeting points between stories of the same series (e.g. the stories of childhood). 'Araby' looks back to 'The Sisters' by alluding to 'the back drawing-room in which the priest had died', while the first three stories have in common a first person narrative in which the 'I' is a young boy who remains unnamed, as if he had not yet qualified for a separate identity.

Resemblances between the stories of adolescence are more a matter of theme than structure; the stories of adult age, however, bring us back to similarities of situations and characters. 'A Little Cloud' and 'Counterparts' can be considered together (because of the final suffering inflicted on a child in both cases). The same applies to 'Clay' and 'A Painful Case', both studies in celibacy, female and male, both— according to certain critics—illustrating the refusal of initiation, whether the rites of Hallowe'en or Isolde's philtre. In the stories of public life, finally, some names recur (in 'Ivy Day' and 'Grace' for instance), while, from the twelfth to the fifteenth piece—that is, if we include 'The Dead'—we are constantly faced with ghosts: Parnell, Madame Glynn ('The ghost of concerts past'), the Holy Ghost of 'Grace' and the ghost of Gretta's first love in 'The Dead'.

Individual structures

Is the unity of *Dubliners* also enforced by a similitude between the structures proper to each individual story? Certain patterns are undoubtedly recurrent. For instance, as the detailed analysis of the stories shows, Joyce had an evident fondness for tripartite divisions— very much like French academics and even more so like the Gaelic writers who invented the 'Triads'. Triads were short poetic and mnemonic statements of the kind:' Three smiles that are worse than grief: the smile of snow melting, the smile of your wife after sleeping with another man, the smile of a leaping dog,' or, 'Three sisters of lying: perhaps, maybe, guess.' In *Dubliners* this tripartite arrangement is some-times secreted by the hero or heroine, as in 'Eveline' where the threefold temporal aspect is a necessity: dreary past, radiant present, impossible future, and is sometimes the outcome of the author's literary formation. Richard Ellmann remarks of Joyce that 'his method of composition was very like T.S. Eliot's, the imaginative absorption of stray material'.* Not only does Joyce remember the masterpieces he has read, but he cannot resist the temptation of pastiche, serious or otherwise; hence, for instance, the triple process of 'Grace', based, it appears, on Dante's *Divine Comedy*, already imitated in 'Clay': *Inferno, Purgatorio, Paradiso*. Sometimes Joyce just unconsciously follows the time-honoured advice that perfection goes by threes: *Omne triduum perfectum*, a Latin saying that was popular in all religious schools. Another recurrent pattern, though perhaps not as frequent as some critics would have it, is the 'epiphany' referred to on page 71 above.

Then, on the level of the texture, a number of stylistic features, characteristic of Joyce's manner in tone and mode, underline in every story his particular type of structure which is generally more lyrical than dramatic.

Such recurrences do not, however, preclude variety. If there is hardly any suspense in *Dubliners* (with the possible exception of 'Two Gallants'), hardly any story in which plot predominates and leads to some sensational revelation or reversal, as with Maupassant, O. Henry or Somerset Maugham (who are not to be despised for this: the 'well-made' short story is no more contemptible than the 'well-made play'), there are differences in action and rhythm between, say, 'Clay' and 'Grace'. There are differences in dimension, which make the first of these stories a mere sketch and 'The Dead' a novella, with a distinct progress in both, linear in the shorter piece, incorporating flashbacks in the longer story. There are differences in winding up and conclusion: none in 'The Sisters', a moral lesson in 'An Encounter', a fit of passionate rejection in 'Araby', contrasted attitudes in 'Eveline', movement and paralysis: 'He rushed beyond the barrier and called her to follow' ... 'Her eyes gave him no sign of love or farewell or recognition'. There is the ironical announcement of daybreak in 'After the race' ... A complete list of variations in dénouement would be too long but attention should be drawn at least to the anti-climax at the end of 'Ivy Day', the comment on a particularly lamentable poem (in spite of the seriousness of the subject): 'Mr Crofton said that it was a very fine piece of writing.'

Differences are to be found even within the same series: those mentioned and others as well. Thus the point of view may vary. The narrator is the same in both 'The Sisters' and 'Araby', but in 'Araby' the world is perceived through a single consciousness while in 'The Sisters' the dead priest's character is successively revealed through the eyes and testimony of several different witnesses according to a method which Henry James (1843–1916) often used.

James Joyce, Oxford University Press, New York, 1959, p.259.

Devastating in his vision, measured in presenting it, for better or for worse, Joyce would soon abandon the discipline learned from the Jesuits in favour of the most unexpected proliferation in English, Irish, or indeed world literature. In *Dubliners*, structural discretion and stylistic tranquillity keep him still for a while in the Society of Jesus.

The texture of *Dubliners*

On the level of texture, to search *Dubliners* for practices common throughout *Ulysses* or *Finnegans Wake* (whose very title is a series of puns on death and life: on death, since this is the funeral wake of Finnegan and *fin*, in French, means 'end'; on life, since the people wake and 'egan' calls 'again' to mind) would be even more absurd than the quest for esoteric symbols or convoluted structures. There is no systematic play on words, no interior monologue or stream-of-consciousness technique proper, and if the spell of verbal magic does begin to be felt by the little boy of 'Two Sisters' and 'Araby' and the adult of 'Counterparts' as well as by the author, all remains subdued.

Language and style; variety

Measure, with Joyce, is no synonym of dullness or poverty, and although the wealth of *Dubliners* is never gaudy, because, in Anthony Burgess's words, 'Joyce is withdrawn, in the post-Flaubertian way',* the collection is rich in original use of the English language.

Phonetics: There are illustrations to be found of the phonetic possibilities of prose. In 'A Mother' Mr Fitzpatrick pronounced the world 'ball' in an Irish, as opposed to English way: 'Mrs Kearney rewarded his very flat final syllable with a quick stare of contempt'. In 'The Dead' 'Gabriel [Conroy] smiled at the three syllables she [Lily] had given his surname.' Here and there, there is an inevitable use of alliteration as in 'A Little Cloud' where Little Chandler, looking at the mean furniture of his house, is reminded of his wife who bought it: 'It too was prim and pretty.' The larger rhythm of the sentence is at times beautifully handled by Joyce, particularly in 'The Dead' (see the opening or the closing paragraph). His direct narrative is matched elsewhere by dialogue or by indirect speech, as, for example, in the sermon of 'Grace': 'He came to speak to business men and he would speak to them in a business-like way. If he might use the metaphor, he said, he was their spiritual accountant.'

Vocabulary: Vocabulary, like grammar, will probably be best considered in another context, although interesting usages of words are to be

---

Joysprick, André Deutsch, London, 1973, p.65.

noticed: adjectives, adverbs, common and especially proper nouns, certain of which are discreetly comic through homophony—for example, in 'After the Race': Ségouin is very similar to 'sagouin' (*French*, bastard); or as in Father Purdon (in 'Grace') through connotation: Purdon Street was renowned for brothels. Others are discreetly symbolical like Gabriel and Michael, the two 'archangels' in 'The Dead'.

Rhetoric: A list of images could easily be compiled here. Some of them are poetical: 'But my body was like a harp and her words and gestures were like fingers running upon the wires' ('Araby'). Some are realistic: 'Corley swung his head to and fro as if to toss an insistent insect' ('Two Gallants'). Some are mock-heroic: 'Mary Jane ... her hands racing along the keyboard or lifted from it at the pauses like those of a priestess in momentary imprecation' ('The Dead').

There are ellipses, for the sake of euphemism—to avoid using too precise a word or vulgar a phrase, like 'die' in the first instance and 'go to hell' in the second: '"Did he ... peacefully?" she asked' ('The Sisters') and '"If he [the priest] doesn't like it," he said bluntly, "he can ... do the other thing"' ('Grace'). There are personifications, like this: 'The other houses of the street, conscious of decent lives within them, gazed at one another with brown imperturbable faces' ('Araby'). There are antitheses, as in the description of Polly, who looked like 'a little perverse madonna' ('The Boarding House').

Language and style; organic adaptation

It would be a mistake, however, to pursue any catalogue however revealing it might be, for in *Dubliners* language and style do not have any isolated finality or value; they are a vehicle of general significance and must therefore be considered in that connection. 'A style of scrupulous meanness'* is, it will be remembered, the phrase Joyce used to describe the manner he chose to further his purpose. The phrase has several meanings:

Precision: It refers, first of all, to a search for realistic (and even down-to-earth) precision that can be illustrated on different planes.

(a) Topographical and chronological minuteness:

> He left his friends at a quarter to ten and went up George's Street. He turned to the left at the City Markets and walked on into Grafton Street ... He went as far as the clock of the College Surgeons: it was on the stroke of ten. He set off briskly along the northern side of the Green ... ('Two Gallants');

*Letter to Grant Richards, 5 May 1906.

(b) Portrait technique with its insistence on ugliness or, at any rate, incongruous or ludicrous elements:

When he smiled he used to uncover his big discoloured teeth and let his tongue lie upon his lower lip. ('The Sisters');

I saw that had great gaps in his mouth between his yellow teeth. ('An Encounter');

His eyes bulged forward slightly and the whites of them were dirty . . . The head itself was so pink and hairless it seemed like a large egg reposing on the papers. ('Counterparts');

His face was fleshy and pallid, touched with colour only at the thick hanging lobes of his ears and at the wide wings of his nose. He had coarse features, a blunt nose, a convex and receding brow, tumid and protruded lips. His heavylidded eyes and the disorder of his scanty hair made him look sleepy. He . . . exploded, before he had well reached the climax of his story, in a kind of high-pitched bronchitic laughter . . . ('The Dead').

A constant search for thoroughness is evident not only in the description of features but of clothes as well:

She had her Sunday finery on. Her blue serge skirt was held at the waist by a belt of black leather. The great silver buckle of her belt seemed to depress the centre of her body, catching the light stuff of her white blouse like a clip. She wore a short black jacket with mother-of-pearl buttons, and a ragged black boa. The ends of her tulle collarette had been carefully disordered and a big bunch of red flowers was pinned in her bosom stems upwards. ('Two Gallants');

His black clothes were tightly buttoned on his short body and it was impossible to say whether he wore a clergyman's collar or a layman's, because the collar of his shabby frock-cloak, the uncovered buttons of which reflected the candle-light, was turned up about his neck. ('Ivy Day');

(c) Lexical accuracy and variety recur in the exploration of certain fields, that of food in particular, which plays such a significant part in 'The Dead' and also in 'The Sisters', 'Two Gallants', and 'A Painful Case', where it is used in a kind of counterpoint to the piece of news that Mr Duffy has just discovered in the paper:

One evening as he was about to put a morsel of corned beef and cabbage into his mouth his hand stopped. His eyes fixed themselves on a paragraph in the evening paper which he had propped against the water-carafe. He replaced the morsel of food on his plate and read the paragraph attentively. Then he drank a glass of water, pushed his plate to one side, doubled the paper down before him between his elbows and read the paragraph over and over again. The cabbage began to deposit a cold white grease on his plate. The girl came over to him to ask was his dinner not properly cooked. He said it was very good and ate a few mouthfuls of it with difficulty. Then he paid his bill and went out.

Such alimentary obsession has also been stressed in Shakespeare's imagery at a period when he obviously wanted to vent his disgust with luxury and materialism, and this perhaps is also the case with Joyce, as we know he was interested in food, and was both a gourmet and greedy.

(d) Capacity to transcribe the variations of speech according to social standing and profession. This is particularly striking with Corley:

It was fine, man—Cigarettes every night she'd bring me, and paying the tram out and back. And one night she brought me two bloody fine cigars—O, the real cheese, you know, that the old fellow used to smoke . . . I was afraid, man, she'd get in the family way. But she's up to the dodge . . . She doesn't know my name. I was too hairy to tell her that. But she thinks I'm a bit of class, you know.'
Lenehan laughed again, noiselessly.
'Of all the good ones ever I heard', he said, 'That emphatically takes the biscuit'. ('Two Gallants').

It is also obvious enough in Gallaher, the successful journalist of 'A Little Cloud'. It denotes age (see the schoolboys' slang in 'An Encounter'); or country: England or, to be precise, London, is on Joyce's linguistic map here (see 'Counterparts'). But particularities of local speech are nearly always popular Irish usages, as in 'Two Sisters': 'Father O'Rourke was in with him *a* Tuesday and anointed him and prepared him *and all*'; 'he looked *that* peaceful and resigned'; 'she's *wore* out'; 'It was *him brought* us all *them* flowers'; 'The duties of the priesthood *was* too much for him'; 'One night he was wanted *for to go* on a call'; '*And what do you think but* there he was . . . *laughing-like* softly to himself'. The same Dublinese occurs in 'Ivy Day': 'I *done* what I could for him, and there he goes *boozing* about'; 'He takes *th'*upper hand of me whenever he sees *I've a sup taken*'; 'Why don't you put him to something?'; 'Sure, *amn't* I never done at the drunken bowsy ever since he left school?'; 'I won't keep you', I *says*.' We see this also with such words as 'shoneens', 'kowtowing', 'spondulicks', or a proverb like: 'The working man gets all kicks and no halfpence,' with interjections like 'musha' or 'usha' or 'wisha'. See also 'A Mother' with the use of 'yo*us*', and 'Grace', 'I know you're a friend of his, not like some of the others he *does be* with.'

Adaptation: Much more than the realistic or naturalistic precision of *Dubliners*, however, what the phrase 'A style of scrupulous meanness' underlines is the translation into words, the adaptation in the style, of the major theme of the work: paralysis and its manifestations or sequels: passivity, narrowness, avarice, and the situations and characters that illustrate it. To start with the latter: the style is sifted often through the perceiving consciousness—Eveline's, for instance, but she is by no means alone, and Zack Bowen has justly remarked:

> Throughout *Dubliners* the narrative point of view, while in the third person, corresponds in tone and phraseology to the state of mind of the central character of each story. Just as the tone of 'Clay' is sweet and naïve, as is Maria, and the tone of 'Counterparts' furious, as is Farrington, so do the breathlessness, excitement and Scott Fitzgerald-like aura of vapid hilarity and derring-do in the narration of 'After the Race' capture the essence of Jimmy Doyle's mood.

Joyce's mimetism can even go further, as is shown in 'The Dead' through the systematic use of adverbs to present Gabriel: 'Gabriel laughed nervously and patted his tie reassuringly'; '... said Gabriel shortly ... said Gabriel awkwardly'; '... said Gabriel moodily'; '... said Gabriel coldly'; 'He stared blankly'.

There is an equally systematic use of the *-ing* form for the spinster-aunts: 'Miss Kate and Miss Julia were there, gossiping and laughing and fussing, walking after each other to the head of the stairs, peering down over the banisters and calling down to Lily to ask her who had come.'

Even more important and frequent is the stylistic formulation of the theme: *visually*, through insistence on darkness rather than light: most scenes are set at night, evening or sunset (see, for instance, 'Eveline', 'A Little Cloud', 'A Painful Case'; and the morning of 'The Dead' erased, as it were, by the fact that it is dark; *intellectually*, through the characters' predilection for clichés, proverbs, set phrases, small talk, conversations on the weather or on ... nothing: 'O, I never said such a thing!' 'O, but you did!' 'O, but I didn't' 'Didn't she say that?' 'Yes. I heard her.' 'O, there's a ... fib!' ('Araby'); or through the narrator's use of key-words (adjectives, nouns and verbs, in that order of frequency) to stress the various states of immobility, impotence, materialism, decadence. Here are some examples:

'The Sisters': an *idle* chalice on his breast
'Araby': air, musty from having been long enclosed. Useless, rusty, feeble
'Eveline': dusty cretonne, tired, broken, close, passive, helpless
'After the Race': stupor
'Two Gallants': streets shuttered for the repose of Sunday, weary harp

'A Little Cloud': stunted houses, mean furniture
'A Painful Case': disused distillery
'A Mother': when the Irish Revival began to be *appreciable*
'Grace': Sacred Heart a *useful* devotion
'The Dead': dull existence, *would*, faintly

Tone

All that we have just explored would be quite sufficient to make *Dubliners* a great work of art, for the closeness between matter and manner gives it organic form, and subdued treatment a classical quality. Yet all that fails to account completely for what *Dubliners* actually is: a collection whose texture sets in relief and yet partly denies its purpose or, at any rate, takes off some of its moral pompousness. For, obsessed as critics have been with Joyce's solemn pronouncements, they have failed to realise that the general tone of the book (tone being another element of texture) was not exclusively, but essentially, of a comic nature. This is hardly true of the childhood episodes, though they are not devoid of irony, nor is it true of 'Eveline'. But immediately after that the comic sets in, remains and—with the sole exception of 'A Painful Case' grows, to reach its climax in 'Grace'—not that 'The Dead' reverses the attitude, but in that story it becomes more internal and turns to humour.

The comic is not only verbal. There is, in 'The Dead' for instance, a comedy of gestures (Freddy Malins running 'the knuckles of his left fist backwards and forwards into his left eye'), of situations (with the total confusion engendered by the different directions given to the cabman), and of character.

This last form (by no means confined to 'The Dead') is, however, on the whole borne by words: it is the language he uses, the little French or Gaelic phrases he introduces in his speech that make Gallaher the pedantic snob he appears to be; it is the repetition of 'To tell you my private and candid opinion', ('Ivy Day') that turns Mr Henchy into a pompous old fool; it is her elocution that makes Madam Glynn ridiculous: 'The poor lady sang *Killarney* in a bodiless gasping voice, with all the old-fashioned mannerisms of intonation and pronunciation which she believed lent elegance to her singing.' ('A Mother').

Properly linguistic instances of the comic rarely include puns other than those occurring in the dialogue, but it is the narrator who plays on the two meanings of 'curate' (assistant parish priest; or barman) on, the connotations of 'pale' (although 'in the pale of' means simply 'within' in other countries, in Ireland it refers to the territories occupied by the English rulers) or on the possible ambiguity of teaching children to play the piano 'at low terms'. All these three examples, however, are taken from 'Grace'; normally puns belong to the characters (like the one on 'brown'), as do other particularities of speech such as Gallaher's half-put-on solemnity when he speaks of 'connubial bliss'; the mother's warped mind finding expression in equally warped syntax: 'My daughter has her contract. She will get four pounds eight into her hand or a foot she won't put on that platform' ('A Mother'); the mispronunciations of Mr Kernan of the injured tongue: 'I' 'ery' uch o'liged to you, sir' ('Grace'); baby-talk, from husbands: 'Nothing for poor little hubby?'* ('Grace'). Finally there are malapropisms such as 'vermin' for 'ermine', 'rheumatic' for 'pneumatic'—not to mention appalling Latin mottoes.

Discreet though he may be, Joyce nevertheless reintroduces himself in a way that greatly enhances the comic value of this book, namely in his comments as author: 'He sat silent for two reasons. The first reason, sufficient in itself, was that he had nothing to say; the second reason was that he considered his companions beneath him' ('Ivy Day'). 'She sat amid the chilly circle of her accomplishments ... trying to console her romantic desires by eating a great deal of Turkish Delight in secret ...' ('A Mother'). 'The concert expired shortly before ten' ('A Mother'). His [Mr O'Madden Burke's] magniloquent western name was the moral umbrella upon which he balanced the fine problem of his finances' ('A Mother'). Some people, however, might prefer to award first prize to the complete sets of pastiches: the patriotic ballad of 'Ivy Day', the sermon of 'Grace', or Gabriel's party speech in 'The Dead'.

Dubliners was described earlier as the epic of a shabby-genteel society. 'Mock-epic' would have been a better term; to use it is not to say anything against the fundamental seriousness of the work: nothing is more serious than the comic, except, perhaps, humour (wit plus love) which triumphs in 'The Dead'.

---

*It is to be remarked, by the way, that this example occurs in a page where there is a reference to Swift, who did not discard that type of self-expression either with Stella or with his other women-folk.

Part 4

Hints for study

General questions

Realism

(1) At the time he was composing the first stories of *Dubliners*, Joyce wrote a sarcastic poem called 'The Holy Office' in which he attacked (once more) the reigning figures of the Irish Literary Movement and stated:

> ... That they may dream their dreamy dreams
> I carry off their filthy streams
> For I can do those things for them
> Through which I lost my diadem,
> Those things for which Grandmother Church
> Left me severely in the lurch.
> Thus I relieve their timid arses,
> Perform my office of Katharsis.

(*a*) What do you think of this idea, that purgative realism should make possible the vague dreams of the Celtic Twilight and be necessary to the current literary fashion?

(*b*) How far does such a statement voice the tone and attitude of the actual stories in *Dubliners*?

(*c*) Ask yourself whether, in *Dubliners*, Joyce is truly a detached, neutral observer or whether he merely pretends to be or plays at being so. Compare 'Eveline' and 'The Dead' in this respect.

(*d*) Watch for—and collate—instances of the author's interventions. Do they amount to some sort of 'message', and if so, what message?

Epiphanies

(1) What are the 'epiphanies' in *Dubliners*?

(2) What mood do they convey (in keeping with or in opposition to the so-called 'realism' or 'naturalism')?

(3) What role do they play?

(4) Do you prefer to consider epiphanies as isolated moments, or do you think, like some critics, that each story is a distinct epiphany?

(5) Taking epiphanies in the first sense above, select one and show how it starts and develops, and whether its style differs in any way from the rest of the story. Say whether it conforms to the description given by Joyce.

Characterisation

(1) Is there a 'main' character in each story?
(2) Select the characters you think most representative. Show and compare their mode of introduction, the way they are set in situation, and their function, and comment on their value as individuals and as dramatis personae.
(3) Would you call Joyce's stories 'psychological'? Why or why not?

Structure and texture

(1) Note down the following elements in each story and try to draw a general conclusion as to Joyce's practice: viewpoint; time pattern; climax; dénouement; language as a means of conveying atmosphere; language as psychological characterisation; language as a class marker; nature of symbols used.

Conclusion

(1) 'Joyce is meticulously controlled, but there is too much art and not enough humanity'. Does this statement reflect your reading of the stories of *Dubliners*?

Questions on individual stories

The Sisters

(1) Structural progression: show in detail the various stages of revelation of the priest's character.
(2) 'Despite his desperate attempts to escape from religion, Stephen's life remains touched by it at all points.' Show how the wealth of religious material in the present story, and even the use of religious language in a secular context, make it possible to apply the quotation to the author himself.
(3) Make a list of the words suggesting a dim, queer and mysterious atmosphere. What reality do they stress?
(4) Make a list of the words suggesting paralysis, decay, evil.
(5) Note down the Irishisms in the story; what role do they play?
(6) What do you think of the ending of the story?

An Encounter

(1) Comment on the function of the following quotations: 'His parents went to eight o'clock mass every morning'; 'The day had grown sultry, and in the windows of the grocers' shops musty biscuits lay bleaching'; 'the squalid streets'; 'The sun left us to our jaded thoughts and the crumbs of our provisions'; 'he was shabbily dressed'; 'He had great gaps in his mouth between his yellow teeth'; 'forced bravery'.

(2) Why is the word 'escape' an important one? Also '*real* adventures'?

(3) How does Joyce convey the man's sadism, and the narrator's ambiguous attitude?

(4) Does the last sentence of the story add anything to it?

Araby

(1) Is not 'waiting', from *Dubliners* to *Waiting for Godot*, a particularly Irish kind of paralysis?

(2) Is there any humour in 'Araby'?

(3) What do you learn in the story of the appearance and life of Dublin at the end of the nineteenth century?

(4) Study the means used by Joyce to convey the hero's impatience.

Eveline

(1) Do you think Joyce's choice of the girl's name has any particular value?

(2) What picture of Eveline's father does the story convey? (Notice what he says as well as what Eveline says of him.)

(3) How is the opposition between change and no change, between fevered action and frozen immobility rendered?

(4) Make a note of what is told in the narrator's voice and in Eveline's voice.

(5) What main attitude towards Eveline in your opinion, does the story leave us with:
detached; ironic; sympathetic; pitying; indifferent?

After the Race

(1) Study the story again as one of 'initiation' where the 'hero' is presented and undergoes an ordeal.

(2) Is there any significance in the proper names given to the various characters?

(3) Make a list of the words implying wealth and attachment to it.

(4) Study the relationship between outside world and plot.

Two Gallants

(1) Show how features, dress, gait and conversation build up a vivid and different picture of each of the two main characters. Does the author intervene? When and how?

(2) How would you define men's attitudes to women in the story? Is there a prevalent one? Do you think Joyce shares it?

(3) Comment on the words used and their repetition: [The harpist] 'plucked at the wires *heedlessly*, glancing ... *wearily* ... at the sky. His harp, too, *heedless* that her coverings had fallen about her knees, seemed *weary* ...'

(4) How does Joyce convey the idea that Lenehan is a failure and the victim of paralysis?

(5) Compare Lenehan's meal and Mr Duffy's in 'A Painful Case'.

(6) Do you think there is a real touch of optimism, a real prospect of betterment in this sentence: 'Experience had embittered his heart against the world. But all hope had not left him'?

The Boarding House

(1) How does Joyce manage to convey the idea that society can force you *physically* as well as *economically* into obeying its rules?

(2) Make a list of all the words relating to military life and warfare. What purpose do they serve?

(3) Study in detail the passage starting: 'she began to reconstruct the interview which she [Mrs Mooney] had had the night before with Polly' and ending with: 'in her *wise innocence* she [Polly] had divined the intention behind her mother's *tolerance*'. Give particular attention to the italicised words, bearing in mind Joyce's pun 'boardelhouse' in *Ulysses*, and that in France *bordels* (brothels) are referred to as *maisons de tolérance* (houses of tolerance).

(4) Comment on the use of the word 'loophole' and make a list of all expressions implying that Doran is about to undergo 'capital' punishment.

A Little Cloud

(1) Comment on the contrasting use of the following words: (a) 'modestly', 'boldly'; (b) 'discreetly', 'gaudy'; (c) 'immoral', 'catholic'.

(2) Make a list of other words (particularly adverbs and occasionally adjectives) used to characterise Little Chandler.

(3) Study Gallaher's way of expressing himself.

(4) Compare the end of 'A Little Cloud' with the end of 'Araby' and of 'Counterparts'.

(5) Will, in your opinion, Little Chandler ever be 'saved'? Comment, in this respect, on the use of the word 'remorse' in the last sentence of the story, bearing in mind E.M. Forster's (1879–1970) comment in *Howards End* (1910):
  'Of all means to regeneration, remorse is surely the most wasteful. It cuts away healthy tissues with the poisoned.'

Counterparts

(1) Study the theme of money in this story.
(2) Study the theme of drink, its causes and effects.
(3) How is the dull routine of Farrington's existence conveyed?
(4) How do the different styles of speech reflect the conflicting forces in 'Counterparts'?
(5) What do you think of Stanislaus Joyce's opinion that 'Counterparts' shows a Russian ability in taking the reader for 'an intercranial journey'?

Clay

(1) What do you think of the sincerity of such phrases as Joe's 'Mamma is mamma, but Maria is my proper mother'?
(2) Study the episode of the gentleman in the tram as Maria's one temptation to face the facts of life.
(3) Compare the structural and symbolic uses of Byron's poem in 'A Little Cloud' with the uses of 'I dreamt that I dwelt in marble halls' in 'Clay'.
(4) Comment on the significance of the anti-climax which serves as dénouement to the story.

A Painful Case

(1) What Nietzschean attitudes do you find in Mr Duffy?
(2) Comment on Joyce's remark that 'He [Duffy] lived at a little distance from his body.'
(3) What do you think of Stephen Reid's statement that 'In psychoanalytic terminology, James Duffy is clearly a compulsion neurotic'?
(4) ... And of Charles D. Wright's view that 'Mr Duffy and Mrs Sinico are both humors characters'?
(5) Study Joyce's pastiche of journalistic style in the paragraph from the *Mail* entitled: 'Death of a Lady at Sydney Parade. A Painful Case'.

Ivy Day in the Committee Room

(1) Make a list of popular and Irish forms and turns of phrase in the canvassers' dialogue.
(2) Is dialogue used here as a means of characterisation? How?
(3) What is the role played by the fire in 'Ivy Day'?
(4) What do you think of Messrs Levin's and Shattuck's opinion that the theme of this story parallels that of Books 13–16 of the *Odyssey*: 'the nation sick with longing for the return of its lost leader'?
(5) Study the story in the light of Hélène Cixous's remark that we find here 'the Lilliputian method of satire at work, reducing everything by reference to a superior, larger being'.
(6) What makes Hynes's poem (*i*) an ambiguous one? (*ii*) a masterpiece of pastiche?

A Mother

(1) Doesn't the name 'Hoppy' Holohan suggest something more than the fact that the character is lame? Also, compare his portrayal in the first and last paragraph of the story.
(2) Make a list of the author's satirical interventions made to ridicule his dramatis personae.
(3) Among such instances, comment on the 'Turkish Delight'; and the phrase: 'After the first year of married life Mrs Kearney perceived that such a man [her husband] would *wear* better than a romantic person'; and ' 'She respected her husband in the same way as she respected the General Post Office, as something large, secure and fixed'.
(4) Comment on the social value of phonetics including the reference to Mr Duggan, 'He said *yous* so softly that it passed unnoticed'.
(5) Consider 'A Mother' as a story of 'public' life in Dublin. How are the public and private aspects of the story related to each other?

Grace

(1) What do you think of the title? Where else in the story do you find the word used, and for what purpose?
(2) Study the first two paragraphs as examples of Joyce's naturalistic method.
(3) In what way does Mrs Kernan's language help to characterise her?
(4) What stand does Joyce take concerning the chauvinism manifested by his characters? ... And concerning their ecumenism?
(5) Can you find any other interpretation of the Biblical passage selected by Father Purdon?

The Dead

(1) How does the first sentence introduce the theme of death?

(2) Locate the instances of humorous or ironical intervention by the author. What role do they play?

(3) Snow is mentioned several times during the story. Look up the instances. What is the effect? Does snow symbolise something, and if so, what?

(4) Study in the same way the mentions of heat, cold, air, fire, rain, dark, light.

(5) On whose side is Joyce? Miss Ivor's? Gabriel's?

(6) Comment on Gabriel's suspicion: 'Perhaps she had not told him all the story'.

(7) What do you think of Frank O'Connor's claim that 'The Dead' is radically different from the other stories in *Dubliners*?

Suggestions for answers

Questions on realism: (1)

At the time he was composing the first stories of *Dubliners*, Joyce wrote a sarcastic poem called 'The Holy Office' in which he attacked (once more) the reigning figures of the Irish Literary Movement and stated:

> ... That they may dream their dreamy dreams
> I carry off their filthy streams
> For I can do those things for them
> Through which I lost my diadem,
> Those things for which Grandmother Church
> Left me severely in the lurch.
> Thus I relieve their timid arses,
> Perform my office of Katharsis.

(*a*) What do you think of this idea, that purgative realism should make possible the vague dreams of the Celtic Twilight and be necessary to the current literary fashion?

(*b*) How far does such a statement voice the tone and attitude of the actual stories in *Dubliners*?

(*c*) Ask yourself whether, in *Dubliners*, Joyce is truly a detached, neutral observer or whether he merely pretends to be or plays at being so. Compare 'Eveline' and 'The Dead' in this respect.

(*d*) Watch for—and collate—instances of the author's interventions. Do they amount to some sort of 'message' and if so what message?

The answer is partly to be found in Richard Ellmann's biography *James*

Joyce, Oxford University Press, New York, 1959, p.171, where 'The Holy Office' is quoted:

> 'The Holy Office' was Joyce's first overt, angry declaration that he would pursue candour while his contemporaries pursued beauty. His short stories, with their grim exactitude and submerged lyricism, had broken away from the Irish literary movement ... As the author of these stories, he was free to attack his literary compatriots for dealing in milk and water which tasted no better for being called Irish and spiritual. For the moment the whole literary movement seemed to him as much a fraud as the Irish virtues, among which cruelty masqueraded as high-minded moralism, and timid onanism masqueraded as purity. One could meet these writers of the 'Revival' and read their works without suspecting that the writers were made of flesh and bone. Joyce's 'holy office', he says, yoking Christian ritual to Aristotle, is 'Katharsis', the revelation of what the hypocritical and self-deceived mummers hide.

Joyce's opinions and reality may not, however, coincide exactly. He was a man of 'counterparts' and therefore tended to define himself *against* things and people, and to attach undue importance to the necessity of contraries—an attitude which made him more Irish than he thought. In fact, if a literary movement may benefit by its opposite, this is by no means a *necessity* for it to survive or prosper.

The 'Celtic Revival' was in no way as ethereal and hypocritical as Joyce implied—any careful reading of, say W.B. Yeats, even in his first manner, will show this. And Joyce himself was far less of a realist or naturalist than he proclaimed: not only did his own poetry fit pretty well in the Irish movement of his time but, even in *Dubliners*, there is an evident liking for 'twilight' landscapes and melancholy recollections, as well as numerous instances of Joyce's cult of beauty.

Questions on characterisation: (1) Is there a 'main' character in each story?

There is a main character in the following stories: the boy in 'The Sisters', 'An Encounter', 'Araby'; Eveline in the story of that name; Little Chandler in 'A Little Cloud'; Farrington in 'Counterparts'; Maria in 'Clay'; Mr Duffy in 'A Painful Case'; and Gabriel in 'The Dead'—in other words, the nine stories in which individual psychology is the essential element, and the viewpoint (in spite of some interventions of the author's) mainly that of one character.

Stories of Dublin 'life' rather than Dubliners' psychology tend, on the other hand, to divide the interest and the point of view between two or more characters and to be organised from the narrator's point of view rather than that of his creations. This is true of 'Two Gallants' (as the title already implies, even though Lenehan is more central to the story than, perhaps, Corley); of 'After the Race'; and still more so, of 'The Boarding House' and 'A Mother'; and above all, 'Grace' and 'Ivy Day in the Committee Room'.

Questions on individual stories: 'Eveline' (1) Do you think Joyce's choice of the girl's name has any particular value?

Clive Hart thinks that the choice of the girl's name is significant. 'Joyce chose Eveline's name with care: she is a little postlapsarian [that is, from after the fall] Eve, remembering happier days while earning her bread in the sweat of her brow'. It is also possible that Joyce wanted to convey the idea that his anti-heroine stood as typical of the whole female condition, by using the name of the first woman.

It is even not unlikely that, remembering the liturgical pun on Eva/Ave (the fallen mother of mankind was saved by the immaculate mother of God, whom the Archangel greeted with the words 'Ave Maria'), Joyce should have chosen the name Eveline as a careful counterpart to the character in 'Clay'—who cannot save anyone (not even herself) because, like Eveline, she is a victim of uncomplaining resignation and a refusal to assume her femininity. Joyce's use of proper names in other stories (Ségouin, Chandler, Duffy, Purdon, and Gabriel, for instance) reinforces the supposition.

Questions on individual stories: 'The Dead' (6) Comment on Gabriel's suspicion: 'Perhaps she had not told him all the story'.

The sentence 'Perhaps she had not told him all the story' should not be divorced from the rest of the paragraph, with its sexual undertones:

> His eyes moved to the chair over which she had thrown some of her clothes. A petticoat string dangled to the floor. One boot stood upright, its limp upper fallen down: the fellow of it lay upon its side.

Gabriel is wondering whether Gretta's relationship with Michael Furey remained as platonic as she said, and he visualises the sexual intercourse she might have had with the young man.

This is exactly what happened to Joyce himself in real life, when Nora had told him of Michael Bodkin (see his letter to his wife in *Selected Letters of James Joyce*, edited by Richard Ellmann, Faber & Faber, London, 1975, p.183). The doubt engendered is full of psychological consequences in that it helps to shatter Gabriel's self-confidence and complacency, thus enabling him to shed the excesses of his egotism— unless it leads him to further exaggerations, like those of Richard, a character in Joyce's play *Exiles*, who was placed in a similar situation:

> I have a deep, deep wound of doubt in my soul ... a deep wound of doubt that can never be healed. I can never know, never in this world. I do not wish to know or to believe. I do not care. It is not in the darkness of belief that I desire you. But in restless living wounding doubt. (*Exiles*, Act 3)

Part 5

Suggestions for further reading

The text

The original version of *Dubliners* by James Joyce was published in London by Grant Richards, 1914.

SCHOLES, ROBERT & LITZ, A. WALTON (eds.): *Dubliners: Text, Criticism and Notes*, The Viking Critical Library, The Viking Press, New York, 1969. This is the best modern edition, but as it is not easily available, the edition used in the preparation of these Notes is:

JOYCE, JAMES: *Dubliners*, Penguin Books, Harmondsworth, 1965; subsequently reprinted. Other editions include:

LEVIN, HARRY (ed.): *The Essential James Joyce*, Penguin Books, Harmondsworth, 1963; American title *The Portable James Joyce*, The Viking Press, New York, 1947, revised 1966; this includes the complete text of *Dubliners* and *Exiles* together with a choice of poems and prose passages.

Criticism of *Dubliners*

BECK, WARREN: *Joyce's 'Dubliners': Substance, Vision and Art*, Duke University Press, Durham, N.C., 1969.

BEJA, MORRIS (ed.): *James Joyce: 'Dubliners' and 'A Portrait'*, Casebook Series, Macmillan, London, 1973.

GARRETT, PETER K., (ed.): *Twentieth Century Interpretations of 'Dubliners'*, Prentice Hall, Englewood Cliffs, N.J., 1968.

GIFFORD, DON: *Joyce Annotated: Notes for 'Dubliners' and 'A Portrait'*, University of California Press, Berkeley, 1982.

HART, CLIVE (ed.): *James Joyce's 'Dubliners'*, Faber & Faber, London, 1969.

MAGALANER, MARVIN: *Time of Apprenticeship: The Fiction of Young James Joyce*, Abelard-Schuman, New York, 1959.

SAN JUAN JR, EPIFANIO: *James Joyce and the Craft of Fiction. An Interpretation of 'Dubliners'*, Fairleigh Dickinson University Press, Rutherford, Madison, Teaneck, 1972.

Other critical works on Joyce

BURGESS, ANTHONY: *Joysprick. An Introduction to the Language of James Joyce*, The Language Library, André Deutsch, London, 1973.

HODGART, MATTHEW: *James Joyce. A Student's Guide*, Routlege & Kegan Paul, London, 1978.

KENNER, HUGH: *Dublin's Joyce*, University of Indiana Press, Bloomington, 1966.

LEVIN, HARRY: *James Joyce: A Critical Introduction*, New Directions, Norfolk, Conn., 1960.

MAGALANER, MARVIN & KAIN, RICHARD M.: *Joyce: The Man, The Work, The Reputation*, Collier Books, New York, 1956.

See also the following collections of critical essays:

BUSHRUI S. B. & BENSTOCK, BERNARD (eds.): *James Joyce: An International Perspective*, Colin Smythe, Gerrards Cross; Barnes & Noble, New York, 1982.

CHACE, WILLIAM M. (ed.): *Joyce. A Collection of Critical Essays*, Prentice Hall, Englewood Cliffs, New Jersey, 1974.

DEMING, ROBERT H. (ed.): *James Joyce, the Critical Heritage*, vol. 1: 1907–27, vol. 2: 1928–41, Routledge & Kegan Paul, London, 1970.

GIVENS, S. (ed.): *James Joyce: Two Decades of Criticism*, Vanguard Press, New York, 1948.

Other works by James Joyce

(a) Publications before 1941:

Chamber Music, Elkin Mathews, London, 1907.

A Portrait of the Artist as a Young Man, Huebsch, New York, 1916. The best modern edition is from The Viking Press, New York, 1964; it is also available in a Penguin Books edition.

Exiles (a play), Grant Richards, London; Huebsch, New York, 1918; Triad/Panther Books, London, 1979.

Ulysses, Shakespeare & Co., Paris, 1922; Penguin Books, Harmonds-worth, 1969.

Pomes Penyeach (poems), Shakespeare & Co., Paris, 1927; Faber & Faber, London, 1933

Collected Poems, Black Sun Press, New York, 1936.

Finnegans Wake, Faber & Faber, London, 1939.

(b) Posthumous publications:

Stephen Hero, edited by Theodore Spencer, New Directions, Norfolk, Conn., 1944, enlarged 1963; Triad/Panther Books, 1977. This is an early draft of *A Portrait of the Artist as a Young Man*.

Epiphanies, edited by Oscar A. Silverman, University of Buffalo, 1956.

Letters, edited by Stuart Gilbert (vol. 1, 1957) and Richard Ellmann (vols. 2 and 3, 1966), The Viking Press, New York; Faber & Faber, London. *Selected Letters,* ibid., 1975.

Critical Writings, edited by Ellsworth Mason and Richard Ellmann, The Viking Press, New York, 1959.

Giacomo Joyce, edited by Richard Ellmann, The Viking Press, New York: Faber & Faber, London, 1968.

General Background

FALLIS, RICHARD: *The Irish Renaissance. An Introduction to Anglo-Irish Literature*, Gill & Macmillan, Dublin, 1978.

MERCIER, VIVIAN: Introduction to *Great Irish Short Stories*, Dell, New York, 1964.

O'CONNOR, FRANK: *The Lonely Voice*, (revised and enlarged), Bantam Books, New York, 1968.

O'FAOLAIN, SEAN: *The Short Story*, (new edition), The Mercier Press, Cork, 1972.

RAFROIDI, PATRICK & BROWN, TERENCE, (eds.): *The Irish Short Story*, Colin Smythe, Gerrards Cross; Humanities Press, Atlantic Highlands, New Jersey, 1979.

REID, IAN: *The Short Story (The Critical Idiom)*, Barnes & Noble, New York, 1977.

Biographies and bibliographies

ELLMANN, RICHARD: *James Joyce*, Oxford University Press, New York, 1959; new and revised edition, 1982.

JOYCE, STANISLAUS: *My Brother's Keeper: James Joyce's Early Years*, edited by Richard Ellmann, preface by T.S. Eliot, The Viking Press, New York, 1958

DEMING, ROBERT H.: *A Bibliography of James Joyce Studies*, University of Kansas Libraries, Lawrence, 1964. To be updated by reading: *Modern Fiction Studies*, 15 (Spring 1969), pp.105–82: and the later issues of *The James Joyce Quarterly*, University of Tulsa.

SLOCUM, JOHN F. & CAHOON, HERBERT: *A Bibliography of James Joyce (1882–1941)*, Yale University Press, New Haven, 1953.

The author of these notes

PATRICK RAFROIDI was educated at the Sorbonne. Agrégé d'anglais, Docteur-ès-lettres, he has taught in Paris, Rouen, Strasbourg, Bloomington and at the University of Lille, of which he is Honorary President. From 1976 to 1979 he was Chairman of the International Association for the Study of Anglo-Irish Literature. He is the founder and chief editor of the yearly journal *Etudes Irlandaises*, and his many publications include: *Irish Literature in English: the Romantic Period, 1789–1850* (1980); he is at present working on a sequel concerning the years 1850–1921. He has also written the York Notes on O'Casey's *The Shadow of a Gunman*. He is now Professor at the University of Paris III – Sorbonne Nouvelle.